A White Man's Country

An Exercise in Canadian Prejudice

A White Man's Country

Doubleday Canada Limited
Toronto

I.S.B.N.: 0-385-11400-1
Library of Congress
Catalog Card Number: 75-18859

Printed in Canada

FIRST EDITION

Printed and Bound in Canada by
T. H. Best Printing Company Limited

To Jessica and Sandy

"That Canada should desire to restrict immigration from the Orient is regarded as natural, that Canada should remain a white man's country is believed to be not only desirable for economic and social reasons but highly necessary on political and national grounds."

MACKENZIE KING,
Deputy Minister of Labor,
in a 1908 report

Author's Note

FROM A DRAMATIC standpoint, the most compelling aspects of the *Komagata Maru* story are the string of murders, the arms-smuggling plots and the voyagers' final clash with the authorities. Yet the uncovering of material on these occurrences was no more fascinating for me than the discovery of hitherto-confidential letters and telegrams and transcripts of conversations with immigration informers. Some of the documents became available by virtue of a 1967 Canadian government edict declaring certain records to mid-July, 1939, were public property. Others came from the private files of H. H. Stevens, the former member of Parliament who had the foresight to hold onto a stack of *Komagata Maru* papers, even notes he had hurriedly scribbled during the 1914 incident.

Stevens and retired Immigration Department employee Fred Taylor provided priceless data on people and specific events. A one-time Ghadrite revolutionary, now in his 90s and wishing to remain anonymous, supplied pertinent information about the party's activities in British Columbia. F. E. Grubb of the B.C. Maritime Museum, Professor N. G. Barrier of the history department, University of Missouri, Michael Halleran of the City of Vancouver Archives, Elizabeth Walker of the Vancouver Public Library's North West history section, and Hong Kong researcher Nancy Dwyer are accorded special thanks.

I am also indebted to *Montreal Star* immigration specialist Sheila Arnopoulos, A. E. Blanchette of the External Affairs Department's historical wing, Anne Yandle of the University of British Columbia's Special Collections branch, Alberta librarians Evelyn Ross and Florence Engler, Ottawa librarian Elizabeth Hunter, Vancouver lawyer F. D. Pratt, G. E. Marrison of the British Museum in London, Roy D'Altroy of the Vancouver Public Library's photo division, Willard Ireland and D. B. Mason of the Provincial Archives in Victoria, S. Chiasson of the Parliamentary Library in Ottawa, the staff of the Public Archives of Canada in Ottawa and Vancouverites R. M. Way, Norman Penny, Don Lang, W. V. Craig and Phil Thomas.

Most of the research for this book was done while I was living in South Vancouver. As the project entailed two years of steady digging, I would like to thank the members of the East Indian community who had the patience and understanding to put up with my seemingly endless questioning.

Ted Ferguson
Westlock, Alberta
May, 1975

A White Man's Country

An Exercise in Canadian Prejudice

Introduction

BRITISH COLUMBIA'S RACIAL strife—and our national shame—had its beginnings during the Cariboo and Fraser gold booms of the 1850s and 1860s. Fifteen hundred Chinese rushed north from United States centers to pan gold and to toil in the newly discovered coal mines. Their pigtails, coolie clothing, language and clannish ways infuriated the white settlers; so did the fact that they would labor long hours for low wages, putting whites out of jobs.

The Chinese community doubled by 1878 and with

the numerical increase came a sharp hike in the white man's resentment. An editorial comment in a Victoria newspaper, the *British Colonist*, echoed the public's anti-Oriental feeling:

"The Chinese ulcer is eating into the prosperity of the country and sooner or later must be cut out."

Instead of removing the "ulcer", the province was to experience its startling growth. The Canadian Pacific Railway was responsible. An estimated 15,000 Chinese were imported at $1 a day (50 cents less than white workers received) to help punch a rail route through the mountains. Between 1881 and 1884 over 10,000 coolies were lured from China and nearly 5,000 from U.S. coastal ports. The usually passive Chinese were taunted into fist fights and, occasionally, more serious altercations with belligerent whites. Yet the racial clashes occurring during the CPR's construction were kids' stuff compared to the violent outbursts that transpired after the Montreal-Port Moody rail link was completed.

The majority of the Chinese railway laborers left the country but roughly 5,000 did not. Staying behind and saving money was the only road open for many coolies who had not earned the price of a China passage. Whenever the employment barometer took a downward plunge, the whites found themselves competing for jobs against the stranded coolies and their newly arrived companions. More often than not, the Orientals won out because, willing to exist on meager diets and in deplorable housing, they could be hired so cheaply.

On January 11, 1887, an embittered mob of 1,000 unemployed Vancouverites marched to a waterfront pier and refused to let 100 Chinese aboard a Hong Kong schooner disembark. Forty-three days later another large mob invaded two Chinese settlements, burning tents and shacks and forcing the occupants to run for their lives, leaving their belongings to the flames.

The following year the provincial government made a bid to curb Chinese immigration with the imposition of a $50 head tax. (The tax was ultimately declared unconstitutional and erased from the law books, only to be resurrected in 1903, this time rising to $500 per person.)

In spite of the head tax and the racial tension, the Chinese kept on coming. No matter how badly Canada treated them, their lot here was an enormous improvement over the grinding poverty of their homeland, where five cents a day was considered good pay. The other nonwhite races joined the immigration flow during the 1890s. The Japanese were right behind the Chinese numerically, and the East Indians were a distant third.

The first East Indians to discover the province's virtues were members of Sikh regiments passing through Canada in 1897 en route home from Queen Victoria's Diamond Jubilee celebration in England. More Sikhs heard tales of the good life at the edge of the Western sea from North Americans fighting in the 1900 Boxer Rebellion. The addition of cheap Japanese and East Indian laborers to the work force stoked the fires of contempt within the white community. The Canadian government managed to achieve a "gentleman's agreement" with Japan, controlling immigration, but no such arrangement could be made with India. The highly esteemed *Pacific Monthly* magazine was one of many publications that preached the open-door policy would result in Canada being flooded by a "brown tide," although fewer than 2,000 East Indians had entered the country at the time. An article printed in 1907 stated:

"Have you ever watched a band of sheep in a rocky and barren field, pasturing until the grass had been eaten down to the roots? You will see the sheep gather near the fence and look longingly at the luxuriant bunch-grass in the next field, while they march back and forth along the fence line in hope of finding a chance to get into the grassy pasture . . .

"India, densely-populated, plague-smitten, famine-stricken, is that over-crowded and over-pastured field; British Columbia and the United States are the green fields toward which the ever-hungry hordes of India are eagerly looking. They have found the gap and are pouring in. Will the rest follow their leaders in an overwhelming flood? Will India, with her 296,000,000 population, of whom more than 100,000,000 are always on the verge of starvation, become an immigration menace? . . ."

The fears of a massive influx of East Indian, Chinese and Japanese newcomers led to the birth of the Asiatic Exclusion League, a racist organization whose membership was an odd blend of jobless workers and some of the province's most prominent business, religious and military leaders.

The league was barely six months old when its spokesmen triggered the worst race riot in Vancouver history, on September 8, 1907. Two factors that set the stage for the riot were the city's temporary economic slump and a sudden spurt in Asian immigration that year. (Eleven thousand Chinese and Japanese entered British Columbia; moreover, 700 East Indians expelled from Washington State had crossed the United States-Canadian border en masse.)

Two thousand league-organized marchers, carrying banners exclaiming *Keep Canada White* and *Stop the Yellow Peril*, descended upon City Hall, then situated on Main Street near the Chinese and Japanese sectors. A series of ranting speeches drew another 3,000 participants and when the angry whites decided to burn B.C. Lieutenant-Governor James Dunsmuir in effigy (Dunsmuir owned coal mines employing Asians) there were 8,000 persons on hand to watch. As night fell, the crowd swelled to 15,000 people. Then after a particularly volatile address by A. E. Fowler, a league zealot who eventually took up residence in a Seattle insane asylum, the mob surged into Chinatown.

The Chinese did not even try to contend with the human bombshell that exploded in their midst. Dozens were beaten and injured, stores were wrecked and plundered, and nobody fought back. The lack of resistance in Chinatown inspired the crowd to continue its rampage in "Little Tokyo." The Japanese, however, were more aggressive and a wild battle ensued. The *Vancouver Province* reported the next day:

"Armed with sticks, clubs, iron bars, revolvers, knives and broken glass, the enraged aliens poured forth into the streets. Hundreds of little brown men rushed the attacking force, their most effective weapons being the knives and bottles, the latter being broken off at the neck, which was held in the hands of the Jap fighter. The broken edges of glass clustering around the necks of the bottles made the weapon very formidable and many a white man was badly gashed about the arms, neck and face . . .

"Armed only with stones, the mob could not stand before the onslaught of knives and broken bottles propelled by the Japanese while they made the air ring with 'Banzais.' Many of the Japanese went to the ground as stones thumped against their heads, but the inscrasible [*sic*] ones were carried off by their friends, and the fight kept up till the mob wavered, broke and finally retreated."

For years the federal government had tactfully side-stepped a head-on confrontation with the immigration issue. West Coast pleas to Prime Minister Sir Wilfrid Laurier had elicited hollow replies promising that the government would study the matter and in due course render a decision.

The 1907 riot made any further avoidance of the problem an impossibility. In its wake, Laurier sent Labor Minister Rolphe Lemieux to Japan for discussions with top-level officials there and Mackenzie King, the Deputy Labor Minister, was dispatched to Vancouver.

On the basis of King's appraisal, the Chinese were awarded $100,000 in compensation and the Japanese an undisclosed amount. And, using Lemieux's and King's reports as guidelines, the Canadian government acted in 1910.

Two orders-in-council were passed. The first declared that all Asians were now obliged to have $200 on their person when they landed. That stipulation dealt a death blow to the system whereby penniless Chinese could repay their fares and meet the $500 head tax requirement once they were employed. The second order-in-council was a regulation designed to stop the East Indians. The regulation specified that East Indian immigrants had to travel directly to Canada from India: however, there were no shipping lines operating between the two countries in those days.

To Stephen Leacock the new law was a nifty bit of bureaucratic footwork. In his historical book, *Canada, the Foundations of the Future*, he wrote: "Hindu immigration to British Columbia was ingeniously side-tracked by the 'continuous journey' rule, as smart a piece of legislation as any that ever disenfranchised negroes in the South. The Hindus were free to come but only on a 'through' ship, and there were no 'through' ships."

Besides the orders-in-council, the Canadian and Japanese governments signed a formal pact limiting Japanese immigration to 400 persons a year. The orders-in-council had their desired impact. Whereas 2,623 East Indians were admitted in 1908, 5 gained entry in 1910, 37 in 1911 and 3 in 1912; all of those allowed in following the adoption of the "continuous journey" regulation were former British Columbians who had already established Canadian domicile and had been visiting their native land.

Chinese and Japanese immigration dried up too, and the federal government smugly thought it had brilliantly eradicated the problem. Not so. A B.C. Supreme Court judge noted for his fair play in labor-management mining disputes, Chief Justice Gordon Hunter, disrupted the governmental calm. In 1913, 36 East Indians turning up in Vancouver aboard a freighter from Singapore were served deportation notices by an immigration official. The East Indians took their case to court. They asked Mr. Justice Dennis Murphy for a writ of *habeas corpus*, claiming they were being illegally detained pending deportation. He dismissed their application, saying he had no right to interfere with an Immigration Act statute.

The 36 then applied to a second judge, Chief Justice Hunter, on the slim chance he would disagree with his bench companion. To everyone's astonishment, he did. The Chief Justice not only ordered the East Indians to be released, he said the 1910 orders-in-council were *ultra vires* because every citizen of India was a British subject and could go anywhere he pleased in the Empire.

The Canadian government was thrust onto the horns of a fresh dilemma. One judge upheld its legislation, another ruled it was invalid. What effect would this have on future immigration? If a test case were to arise, would the court support Murphy or Hunter? In a jittery bid to shore up the Immigration Act, the government hastily passed a new order-in-council making it illegal for artisans or laborers, skilled or unskilled, to enter Canada at any sea terminal in British Columbia.

It was against this backdrop of racial turmoil and legal confusion that the *Komagata Maru* wove her tapestry of death and deceit and, in the process, bequeathed white Canadians an enduring legacy of shame.

On May 22, 1914, the day before the *Komagata Maru* was to arrive in Vancouver, prejudice against nonwhites was again running high. A murder trial festering with racial overtones had just concluded.

A 16-year-old Chinese houseboy, Jack Kong, had slain his employer, Mrs. Clara Millard, in a dispute over a bowl of porridge. Mrs. Millard had cast slurs on the breakfast cereal Kong had cooked, and when she threatened to slice off his ear he beat her to death with a dining room chair. Kong drew a life sentence, a penalty the anti-Asian elements denounced as far too merciful.

To make matters worse, Vancouver was in the midst of yet another labor crisis. Not that the city showed many signs of the employment slump that had thousands queuing up at slum-area soup kitchens and breadlines.

Electric streetcars and smart automobiles like the Chandler ("It has climbed every demonstrating hill from coast to coast," the ads boasted) scooted along 49 miles of paved roads. Housewives wore ankle-hugging cotton dresses sporting silk collars and cuffs on shopping excursions, while businessmen in finely tailored three-button suits and matching vests closed deals in a downtown district steadily thickening with a crop of stone and concrete skyscrapers.

The most impressive of all the structures was the 14-story Dominion Trust Building, the tallest edifice in the British Empire. Its cream-and-rose coloring and its red granite pillars, imported from Scotland, delighted passers-by. Other eye-pleasers were the plush-seated Empress Theatre (the electrifying Melba and a dog act once shared the same bill there) and the elegantly furnished Hotel Vancouver. The hotel's rooftop tea garden and its deep-cushioned bamboo chairs vied for popularity with the tearooms at David Spencer's department store where wall signs assured customers, "Every piece of crockery will be sterilized by modern machinery after use."

Charity balls, debutante rituals and champagne parties enthralled inhabitants of posh Shaughnessy Heights. So did the exploits of the devilish Charlie Henshaw: he shocked the town when the chemically treated bathing costumes he loaned guests at a party aboard his yacht disintegrated in the water. In a less puckish vein the amusements that summer included listening to ragtime pianists, watching Mack Sennett films or swaying in a lawn hammock plucking an off-key mandolin.

But the exuberance and affluence of a fast-expanding lumber, mining and seaport center—Vancouver's population had risen to 207,383—was confined almost exclusively to the upper and middle classes. A hefty portion of the working-class community was in dire straits. During two prosperous years, 1911 and 1912, the city had opened its arms to laborers from Great Britain, Continental Europe, the United States and other parts of Canada. In the winter of 1913, however, the workers greatly outnumbered the available jobs. By the spring of 1914 Vancouver's relief rolls were stretched to the limit, a condition that was to last until late 1915, when the city was blessed with a cascade of war-generated government contracts.

The press and the politicians did not blame the province-wide labor quandary wholly on their usual whipping boy, the nonwhites; but both sources did claim the Asians' willingness to work for scanty wages was a major contributing factor. For weeks before the *Komagata Maru* appeared, Vancouver newspapers carried telegraph stories from Hong Kong, Shanghai and Yokohama warning that a boatload of job-hungry Punjabis were bound for B.C.'s shores. On the night the freighter put in to port B.C. Premier Sir Richard McBride, speaking of Asian immigration in general, told a *Times* of London correspondent:

"To admit Orientals in large numbers would mean in the end the extinction of the white people, and we always have in mind the necessity of keeping this a white man's country."

One

THE *KOMAGATA MARU* was an eyesore. The paint was peeling on her funnel and deckhouse, there were forlorn rusty patches on her sides, and her brown canvas awnings, strung about the deck to provide shade during hot spells, were frayed and sun-bleached.

The 2,900-ton freighter was past her prime in seaworthiness too. Although only 17 years old, she had been allowed to deteriorate by several unconcerned masters since she left her original owners, Hamburg-American Lines, nine years earlier and commenced service in the

Far East. The vessel's once gleaming and efficient steam engine was now such a grimy, temperamental machine that many merchants would not charter her.

The *Komagata Maru*'s multiple deficiencies did not perturb Gurdit Singh: his objective was to find a vessel capable of transporting 500 passengers. The tramp steamer resting at anchor in Hong Kong harbor fit the bill nicely. Granted, some people might disdain the passenger accommodations—rows of communal bunks hacked out of rough lumber and crammed into the steerage section— but he felt sure that the voyage he was proposing would have potential customers clamoring for tickets.

What the white-bearded, turbaned Sikh had in mind was to lead an expedition of his oppressed tribesmen, the East Indians, to a 20th-century "promised land," British Columbia. Gurdit's motive was financial, not spiritual. A successful businessman, he had fallen under the spell of the commercial world's most seductive siren, the prospect of bigger profits. Closing down his contractor's office in Singapore in March, 1914, he traveled to the British colony and chartered the *Komagata Maru*. His eight-year-old son, Balwant, and his male secretary, Daljit Singh, accompanied him.

The charter was easily arranged. A German-born shipping agent living in Hong Kong signed a six-month contract with Gurdit on behalf of the ship's Japanese owners, the Shinei Kishen Go Shi Kaisha Company. The East Indian made a substantial down payment (the exact sum is not known) and promised to pay the outstanding $22,000 when the freighter reached Vancouver.

Forming the Sri Guru Nanek Steamship Company (named after the founder of the Sikh faith), Gurdit proceeded to sell tickets and shares in the heavily populated East Indian quarter. Though unimpressive physically—he was a short, thick-chested, slightly stooped man of 55—Gurdit was a quick-witted charmer who rarely failed to draw people—and their money—to him. Within a week he sold nearly $5,000 worth of stock and fares and he had gotten a Hong Kong merchant's agreement to purchase the B.C. lumber he planned to transport on the *Komagata Maru*'s return voyage.

Gurdit's winning image was greatly enhanced by his scholarly, patriarchal manner. The East Indians he was enticing into the venture were mostly younger men of limited education: to them he was a superior being deserving of respect.

Born and raised in Amritsar, the Sikh holy city in the Punjab, Gurdit had attended British-run schools up to university level; he liked to quote Dickens and Byron and his mathematical wizardry awed those poor souls among his clientele who were still struggling with the multiplication table. From a business viewpoint, however, Gurdit's finest asset was not his arithmetical aptitude: it was the training he had acquired in his father's pawnshop. As a youth Gurdit often stood behind the counter haggling with everyone from old Etonians down on their luck to hard-core criminals peddling goods of dubious origin. It was here that he honed his persuasive charms to near-perfection and it was here that he developed his life-long passion for the bewitching dollar.

Gurdit's occupations varied. He was a building and railway contractor, a bookstore owner, a linen exporter and, treading in his father's tracks, a pawnbroker. He succeeded at all these activities, but his supreme goal—enormous wealth—always eluded him. The *Komagata Maru* enterprise would, he hoped, help remedy that condition. He envisioned a fleet of Sri Guru Nanek freighters carrying passengers and cargo between British

Columbia and Far Eastern points. Two a month by the
end of the year, one a week eventually. He was confi-
dent that Canada's immigration laws would collapse the
moment the *Komagata Maru* sailed into Vancouver
harbor: after all, the passengers were British subjects
and nothing short of India's gaining independence or
another foreign power's seizing control of the country
could obliterate that fact.

The Hong Kong police saw things differently. On
March 24 Gurdit was arrested and charged with selling
tickets for an illegal voyage. He immediately contacted
two Queen Street law partners who went to the police
station bearing a letter stating the authorities had no
right to keep the *Komagata Maru* from leaving Hong
Kong. The letter said:

". . . In our opinion there are no restrictions upon the
immigration by Indians from the Colony unless they are
under contract of service. [Immigrants whose fares are
paid by employers if they sign long-term contracts and
repay the money in weekly installments.] No immigrants under contract of service can leave the Colony by
any ship carrying from Hong Kong more than 20 passengers who are natives of Asia without complying with
certain provisions in the Chinese Immigration Ordinance. We are therefore of the opinion that any Indians
can leave the Colony for any destination unless they are
bound by contract of service."

The police conceded that the document accurately
interpreted the local regulation governing departing vessels. But what about Asian ships arriving in Canada? Was
it not their duty, in the interest of Empire solidarity, to
do whatever they could to prevent trouble in His
Majesty's North American territory? The lawyers retorted that, quite frankly, Canada's internal affairs were

none of the Hong Kong police department's business. And, they added, if the *Komagata Maru* did not sail, Gurdit Singh would launch a million-pound damage suit against the Hong Kong government. Both parties dug in their heels, anticipating a lengthy and arduous legal scrap. Gurdit Singh was released on bail and the *Komagata Maru* was placed under police guard.

Much to their dismay, the police officials learned that the "continuous journey" edict they based their case upon was tottering on a shaky foundation. The Colonial Secretary wired Ottawa explaining the colony's predicament and asking the Canadian government either to sanction the *Komagata Maru* expedition or to supply the legislative ammunition for a court battle. If Ottawa had fired off a firm reply, standing behind its immigration laws, it could have kept the ship in Hong Kong indefinitely, a victim of the colony's slow-moving legal system. It procrastinated instead. After waiting six days for an answer that never came, the Colonial Secretary informed the police department it had insufficient grounds for holding the freighter. The charge against Gurdit Singh was dropped, the police withdrew their shipboard guards, and the Canadian government, through its own lack of decisive action, missed a perfect chance to avert the whole *Komagata Maru* tragedy.

Not surprisingly, the unfavorable publicity surrounding Gurdit's arrest hurt ticket sales. Although they liked and admired him personally, the East Indians refused to part with their money until Gurdit could prove they would be admitted to Canada. Even worse, shareholders and people already possessing tickets were on the verge of demanding refunds.

The fact that no bona-fide proof existed did not deter the resourceful Sikh. In the office of the passage broker he spied a stack of the white tickets that served as contract-of-service pacts between Chinese coolies and overseas employers. One reading of the English wording on the slips—a perplexing arrangement of lawyers' mumbo-jumbo—told Gurdit they could conceivably pass for landing papers. With regenerated vigor, he stuffed the pockets of his natty tweed suit with the coolie tickets and resumed his sales campaign in the East Indian quarter.

Distributed along with the blue passage tickets, the white slips dispelled the qualms of passengers and shareholders alike. One hundred and sixty-five persons bought berths in Hong Kong, and Gurdit expected to hit his 500-passenger target during stop-overs in three Asian ports.

Financially, the Sri Guru Nanek Steamship Company was in splendid shape. The fares sold at $100 apiece, twice the cost of a third-class berth on a Canadian Pacific liner. (The passengers gladly paid the exorbitant fee because the CP steamers would not allot space to an East Indian unless he had acquired Canadian domicile.) The cash flow from investors and the profit from a coal consignment Gurdit planned to unload in Vancouver matched the charter price. All of the fare money and the proceeds from the lumber the ship was bringing back would be frosting on the cake.

On the morning of April 4 the rusty freighter fired its boilers and churned out of Hong Kong harbor, moving north along the China coast. Gurdit had placed advertisements in Shanghai, Moji and Yokohama newspapers trumpeting his company's maiden effort, but the printed fanfare did not swell the passenger ranks to the 500 mark. When the *Komagata Maru* headed across the immense Pacific, there were 376 ticket-holders aboard:

111 had joined the ship at Shanghai, 86 at Moji and 14 at Yokohama.

With the exception of 17 Muslims, the passengers belonged to the Sikh religion. Nearly all of them, Sikhs and Muslims, were farmers who had laid down their hoes and picked up British Army rifles. Their two-year military hitches over, they did not want to go back to India until they could afford to buy oxen or to finance irrigation systems conveying new life to parched soil. The dazzling bait of British Columbia's riches induced many passengers to borrow heavily from East Indian and Chinese money-lenders; to the proud Sikhs, death would be an attractive proposition compared to the humiliation of returning to the Orient under the yoke of a crushing debt.

The Sikhs came from the Punjab, a largely arid and treeless plain in northern India. Their faith forbade them to consume alcohol, smoke tobacco, commit adultery, eat an animal that had been slowly bled (a Muslim custom) or cut any hair on their body (a symbol of religious devotion).

Originally a pacifist sect, Sikhism developed a militaristic bent in the 1600s as a defense against Hindu and Muslim persecution. A baptismal ceremony was initiated at which Sikh males were given the "family" name Singh, a Punjabi word meaning "lion". It was also decreed that all Sikh men would carry swords, wear knee-length military breeches and resort to violence when all other methods failed.

The Sikhs' militarism helped save them from possible annihilation in the 1720s-1730s. A Muslim governor ordered the massacre of every Sikh man, woman and child in the Punjab. Thousands were put to death daily and a reward was paid for every head brought to the governor's headquarters. The Sikhs formed guerrilla bands and survived the extermination plan.

Driven by religious fervor, the average Sikh warrior was a ferocious creature in combat—a fact that became painfully clear to the British during the Anglo-Sikh wars. In 1846 the largest English army ever mustered in India, 40,000 troops, was needed to gain control of the Punjab. Three years later the Sikhs rebelled and the British had to assemble another huge force, 50,000 men, to quell them. D. A. Sanford said in his account of the second Anglo-Sikh campaign: "The Sikhs fought like devils . . . untamed even in their dying struggle . . . they ran right on the bayonets and struck their assailants when they were transfixed."

The Sikhs aboard the *Komagata Maru* did not have to face any bayonets on the Pacific crossing, but a certain amount of their celebrated grit and determination was required to endure the appalling living conditions.

The ventilation in the bunk-filled steerage section was so bad dozens of passengers preferred to sleep on the open deck, although they had only a single blanket to cover them. There were not enough toilets or washing facilities and the few that did exist were filthy. The ship reeked of curry: the passengers cooked their meals (mostly potato soup, curried rice and pancakes) on the deck in big cast-iron pots.

On May 21 the *Komagata Maru* ended a dreary seven-week voyage with the sighting of the B.C. coast. The passengers swarmed around the railing, talking excitedly, their eyes and thoughts on the craggy, tree-bunched shores of Vancouver Island. An immigration pilot boarded the freighter at sunset and took her to the William Head quarantine station where she lay overnight.

At seven o'clock the next morning a government medical officer, a Japanese interpreter and an immigration officer went on board. The doctor learned that neither the ship's Japanese master, Captain Yamamoto, nor the ship's physician, Dr. Raghunath Singh, had obtained an official bill-of-health clearance for the passengers before leaving the Far East. He vaccinated everyone on board and the freighter left for Vancouver, 37 miles away, that evening.

A Canadian pilot guided the ship across the choppy Strait of Georgia. At midnight the *Komagata Maru* rounded the dark bulge of Point Grey, passed Stanley Park and sheared into Burrard Inlet: by 12:30 A.M., May 23, the dingy freighter was riding at anchor at the foot of Burrard Street, about a mile from the core of the slumbering city.

Two

BY MID-MORNING a human wolfpack prowled the waterfront.

Drifting back and forth between harbor pubs and Pier A, the wharf closest to the *Komagata Maru*, several hundred unemployed workers indulged in a day-long hostility session, shouting insults and waving clenched fists at the "Hindu invaders." Fortunately, a slash of cold sea water, approximately 200 yards in width, separated the East Indians and their white antagonists: acting on Immigration Department orders, the pilot had anchored the vessel away from the dock to discourage ship-jumpers. The government launch *Winimac* was also on hand. With two armed immigration agents on board, the *Winimac* had begun a watch-dog patrol around the *Komagata Maru* the moment her twin flukes burrowed into Burrard Inlet mud. A second launch, the *Mary Ellen*, was to spell the *Winimac* every 12 hours.

The hostile mob placed its hopes for the freighter's rapid expulsion upon the sturdy shoulders of Inspector Malcolm Reid, the Immigration Department's Vancouver supervisor. When he strode down Pier A at 10 A.M. he was greeted by pleas to "Drive the beggars back to the Ganges."

Reid cut a robust, manly figure in his dark-blue uniform and cap. His handsome head was borne atop a muscular, six-foot-plus frame held ramrod-straight. His bushy mustache had waxed and pointed tips, his graying hair was neatly cropped, and when he spoke to the laborers on the wharf, assuring them that most of the passengers would be deported, his voice was full-bodied and authoritative.

Reid's dashing bearing belied his true character. A 38-year-old Presbyterian Scot, he was humorless, thrifty, obstinate and, in the opinion of former immigration staffer Fred Taylor, an insecure person with a near-crippling dread of anything not covered by a government regulation.

Teaching had been Reid's initial career. A coal miner's son, he taught at the elementary level in the Yukon and in Vancouver before joining the Immigration Department in 1911. That same year he became an original member of the Seaforth Highlanders' local reserve (he was part of the Canadian contingent participating in King George V's coronation ceremony) and he owed his superb physical condition to regular drills at the Seaforth encampment.

He owed something else to the Highlanders too. A senior officer's advice on how to appear calm under pressure had served him well in his immigration work. Now it would serve him again. Leaving the disgruntled laborers, Reid walked to the end of Pier A where six immigration men had gathered. The six included Taylor and immigration medical officer Dr. A. S. Monro. In 1974 Taylor, a lucid and engaging 90-year-old, described what occurred when the *Winimac* carried the boarding party to the freighter:

"I was a bit apprehensive because I didn't know what to expect. Reid, of course, was going by the rulebook. Those who couldn't prove Canadian domicile would be deported. And, judging by Far East reports, that meant just about every passenger on the boat. But the regulation Reid was relying upon was in jeopardy. What would happen if he ordered the ship to leave and it stayed put? A lot of the passengers had fought in the British Army and we knew they could give us a real bad time if we tried to push them around.

"The East Indians rushed to our side of the freighter as we approached. Hundreds of faces peered down at us. Some were smiling; they thought we were coming to tell them they could land.

"Reid went up the gangway and we followed. Gurdit Singh's secretary, Daljit Singh, met us and said his boss was at prayer. He was a slim, gentle fellow, about 30 years of age, and like Gurdit Singh he spoke excellent English. While we talked to Captain Yamamoto through an interpreter, Daljit had some passengers line up for a medical examination.

"There were four children and two young wives on board. Three of the kids and both women were eventually permitted to disembark. The fourth child was

Gurdit Singh's son. The men were dressed in their best suits and ties, all very fashionably British, and their bags were packed. Every passenger was ready to go ashore at a moment's notice."

For most of them, that notice never came. Reid and his associates determined that 22 people could claim Canadian domicile. For the remaining passengers, the coolie tickets Gurdit Singh had provided in Hong Kong were utterly useless. When he emerged from below deck in the early afternoon, Gurdit passed the word amongst his flock that the Canadian government had changed the regulation governing the white tickets without his knowledge. His explanation was accepted.

Gurdit's verbal magic placated the passengers but it had no effect whatsoever on Reid. Walking to the table set up outside the wheelhouse where Reid sat examining documents, the stocky Sikh smilingly asked why so many people were being denied entry to Vancouver. Because, Reid replied coldly, they were in the country illegally.

Stroking his flowing snow-white whiskers, Gurdit quietly protested that Reid was mistaken—they were all British subjects, were they not? The inspector abruptly switched arguments. Each passenger was required to have $200 cash on his person, he said, and the majority of Gurdit's charges obviously did not have the money. No problem, Gurdit said. Once he got ashore he would collect it from the local East Indian community. That would be impossible, Reid replied, because he would never tread on Canadian soil.

Up to that point their exchange had been relatively cordial: Gurdit was friendly and tactful, Reid firm and polite. The inspector's declaration that Gurdit was banned from entering Canada exposed one of the patriarchal Sikh's prime weaknesses, a volcanic temper. Yelling and gesturing, he swore every passenger on the boat would land if they had to fight their way into the city. Leaving the threat to sink in, Gurdit stomped across deck, criticizing the "stupid white man's government" for the benefit of every Punjabi within earshot.

Reid treated Gurdit Singh's flare-up as though it had not taken place. With the detached air of a schoolteacher marking exam papers, he returned to his inspection of the passengers' personal documents. When he was finished, Reid and his men left the ship. An hour after they got off, three immigration officers, holstered pistols on their hips, boarded the *Komagata Maru.* Gurdit's threat had indeed sunk in. Reid was assigning guards to the freighter in eight-hour shifts: an added bit of insurance against ship-jumping attempts.

Later that evening Gurdit persuaded a Japanese crewman to take a note to Sikh Temple secretary Mit Singh. (Captain Yamamoto and his crew could come and go as they pleased, using the government launches as ferries.) In the note, Gurdit outlined the passengers' plight and inquired if Mit knew the name of a good lawyer. Mit instantly telephoned Edward J. Bird, a glib attorney whose enthusiasm for underdog causes equaled his zeal for fancy clothing.

Bird was given a tough challenge. He was to represent the passengers in a court fight aimed at testing the vulnerability of the Immigration Act. Because the federal government would be extremely eager to win the case, Bird's legal opponent was bound to be a seasoned and skilled practitioner.

Two days later, on May 24, the paunchy, middle-aged Bird went to Malcolm Reid's office on the top floor of the Immigration Building, a decrepit two-story frame structure on Burrard Street, a stone's throw from Pier A. It was small, cramped and, contradicting its occupants' spic-and-span appearance, an unsightly mess. Files, memos, letters, telegrams and yellowing old newspapers were piled atop a filing cabinet, a square oak desk and a dusty bookcase. One pale green wall held a bright Union Jack, another a soiled map of the world. The window behind the desk was the room's sole appealing feature: it offered a stirring view of the harbor and the evergreen-pocked North Shore mountains across the mile-and-a-half-wide Inlet. In the foreground was the gently riding hulk of the *Komagata Maru*.

Bird leapt right to the point. He had dropped in to clear up a minor formality: he needed the inspector's permission to confer with Gurdit Singh aboard the freighter. Reid said he did not think Bird's request was merely a minor formality. In fact, he considered it vitally important that no one be allowed on the ship except immigration personnel. He had detected a potentially explosive situation, he said, and he did not want any East Indian sympathizers—lawyers or anyone else—smuggling guns to the passengers.

Bird was astonished. He suspected the white community distrusted him for defending social rejects (native Indians and East Indians among them) but, he said, he had never been cast in the role of a criminal accomplice. Besides, he added, under the Canadian judicial system, an attorney had every right to have a private consultation with his client. That might be so in most instances, Reid stated, but this was a special case demanding special measures.

Unknowingly copying Gurdit Singh's angry exit, Bird walked out of the office in a huff. He would inform Reid's superior in Ottawa, immigration superintendent

W. D. Scott, about the inspector's "idiotic" restriction, he said as he left, and if Scott supported Reid, then he would demolish the ban with a court order.

(A career civil servant, Scott's pro-white bias was well-known. Noting that a large number of American blacks had migrated to the Prairies, he wrote in a 1914 government publication that it was "to be hoped that climatic conditions will prove unsatisfactory to those new settlers, and that the fertile lands of the West will be left to be cultivated by the white race only.")

Reid and Dr. Monro departed for the *Komagata Maru* at noon. The futility of taunting the unwanted Punjabis from a distance had reduced the previous day's Pier A mob to an occasional spectator. On board the ship, Reid began compiling a bulky file listing the passengers' names, occupations, ages and places of birth. Gurdit and Reid hardly spoke to one another, and when they did the conversation was strained and terse. While Reid put his file together, Dr. Monro examined passengers. The language barrier and the Asians' fears that by co-operating fully they might be signing their deportation warrants stretched both chores into week-long struggles. (Dr. Monro ultimately reported that 90 passengers were physically ill and should be deported on those grounds alone. The most common ailment was trachoma, a highly contagious virus.)

Bird meanwhile dispatched a wire to Scott. He mentioned the possibility of a court order and said he was on the verge of launching a damage suit against the federal government.

The May 24 edition of the *World*, a Vancouver evening daily, attributed this statement to Bird:

"The immigration service is exceeding its authority and is endeavouring to import Russian government methods into this country in order to keep out British subjects. There are no laws which permit the immigration officials to act as they have in the case of the *Komagata Maru*. The officers have taken armed possession of the ship and have guards patrolling the waters around her in launches, preventing anyone from boarding or leaving the vessel."

The *Komagata Maru* was shunted off the front pages the following day. The Sells Foto Circus bounded into town and Vancouverites jammed city streets to see a dazzling parade spotlighting that star of stars, Buffalo Bill Cody. Only the morning *Sun* allotted space to the freighter, a page-10 story headed "Nothing New In Hindu Conspiracy." (The local press labeled all East Indians "Hindus" although the Sikhs lavished little love on the Hindu religion.)

The word had not yet reached the newsrooms but something new had taken place behind the scenes. The federal government had picked the man it was sending up against Edward Bird. He was a genial, bespectacled, slightly built legal veteran named Robie Reid. Bird and Reid were total opposites, professionally and privately. Whereas the Sikhs' lawyer had a soft spot for the underdog, Reid was partial to Establishment clients. Bird was a veritable fashion plate, while Reid was a conservative dresser, preferring gray suits. And whereas Bird's rapier tongue was his best weapon in court, Reid's forte was thorough research and a phenomenal knowledge of the law.

Robie Reid was a natural choice: he had often represented the Justice Department on the West Coast, and Ottawa knew from experience how proficient he was. In accepting the assignment, he was given explicit instructions on how to proceed. These instructions originated

with Sir Robert Borden, the shy Nova Scotia lawyer
who had wrested the Prime Minister's mantle from Sir
Wilfrid Laurier in 1911.

Borden wanted him to have the assault on the Immigration Act restricted to a single test case. As the law stood,
all 354 passengers could submit individual applications
for entry to the Immigration Department's five-man
Board of Inquiry. If rejected, each applicant could file for
a writ of *habeas corpus*, charging he was being illegally
detained. Not only that, but each passenger could file
habeas corpus with all seven judges of the B.C. Supreme
Court, one judge at a time. Under those circumstances,
it might take years to resolve the *Komagata Maru* issue.

On May 27 Reid and Bird met at the latter's office
and Reid proposed the single test case. Writing in the
January, 1941, edition of the *B.C. Historical Quarterly*,
the government attorney commented upon Bird's reaction to this:

"Mr. Bird was satisfied with our proposal but it was
necessary for him to obtain the approval of his clients
before giving his formal consent. He was evidently confi-
dent that they would concur for on May 28 he told a
reporter of the course which had been agreed upon, and
apparently took considerable credit to himself for
having the matter arranged in this way."

Bird's confidence was ill founded. When he had the
Winimac deliver a letter to Gurdit Singh defining
Borden's terms, the East Indian leader fired back a
heated reply spurning them outright. The passengers
demanded justice in the normal manner, Gurdit wrote.
Therefore all 376 of them—even those with Canadian
domicile—wished to have individual Board of Inquiry
hearings and, if need be, to go on to face the seven
Supreme Court judges.

Gurdit was bidding for time. At that moment he had no tactical cards to play, but there was always the chance he would find a few if the Appeal Court was denied the opportunity to bring down what he figured would be a swift deportation verdict.

So unless someone—Robie Reid, Bird, the Prime Minister, anyone—could convince Gurdit Singh otherwise, the *Komagata Maru* conflict was going to be tediously long and enormously complicated.

Three

"Then let us stand united all
  And show our father's might,
  That won the home we call our own,
  For white man's land we fight.
  To Oriental grasp and greed
  We'll surrender, no never.
  Our watchword be God Save The King
  White Canada Forever."

THE SONG WAS entitled "White Canada Forever." A music hall favorite in 1906, it enjoyed a

short-lived comeback in Vancouver during the hot and hectic summer of 1914.

The anonymous author's inspiration is not known, but it could very well have been the hate-mongering articles appearing in the daily newspapers. Since the *British Colonist*'s "Chinese ulcer" smear in 1878, the B.C. press had periodically depicted all nonwhite immigrants as loathsome, barbaric creatures. The arrival of the *Komagata Maru* heralded a new outburst of anti-Asian newspaper propaganda. This campaign became particularly vicious after Gurdit Singh announced his intention to assail the Immigration Act.

The *Sun* lashed out with sharper claws than any of its competitors saw fit to use. On June 3, 11 days after the freighter anchored, the paper carried an un-bylined page-two story, "The Other Side of the Hindu Curtain," which claimed "the East Indian relishes the clandestine and the surreptitious. Anything done in the dark or from ambush is fascinating. He lusts for mystery and skulking . . . If the Hindu conspirators hatch a plot today, the drift of gossip in the air tomorrow carries news of it. Their tongues are like those of scandal-thinking women."

And as if that was not poisonous enough, the *Sun* published a companion piece, "Hindus Cherish No Amity for Whites," in which a reporter assuming the pseudonym Pollough Pogue recounted a chat between himself and an unnamed Sikh firebrand.

"The old man was a tiger. His words were flames and blood. He spat as he spoke of the immigration officials. He gnashed his teeth as he spoke of the government. He said the people on the *Komagata Maru* would land and more would come. If I were to write down what he said about the white race, it would cause a riot. I have heard

Hindus talk about assassinating white officials and burning Vancouver, but I have never heard anything half as bad as that old man said."

In response to the rising tide of opposition among whites and worried about the passengers' plight, the Temple Committee was formed. Priests Bhag Singh and Balwant Singh, and Hoosain Rahim, editor of a monthly journal, *The Hindustanee*, were the driving forces behind its foundation. The committee grew out of a series of letters between Gurdit Singh and Bhag, the most influential priest at the Sikh Temple.

Malcolm Reid had granted the passengers permission to send and receive mail via the government launches, and Gurdit had taken advantage of the communications outlet to besiege Bhag with requests for financial aid. Because the immigration inspector refused to let the freighter tie up at a dock and unload her coal cargo, Gurdit wrote, he could not acquire the funds to erase the $22,000 charter debt. Then, too, there was Bird's fee: the passengers would surely lose his services if they did not pay him, and, unless some dollars fell from the sky, it was unlikely they would ever have the means to do so. The 15-member committee agreed to meet both obligations.

Although Bhag and Rahim's motives were purely charitable at the time of the committee's formation, these two were not merely concerned countrymen of the prisoners aboard the *Komagata Maru*. In addition to their respected public positions within Vancouver's East Indian community, they belonged to a secret terrorist organization, the *Ghadr*. Both men set out to solve the dispute with the immigration authorities in a legal and peaceful manner. Should the diplomatic approach fail, however, they were prepared to turn the matter over to their Ghadrite comrades.

On the evening of June 3, 600 East Indians contributed $5,000 in cash and $50,000 in pledges at a committee-sponsored meeting held at a rented hall. Following brief speeches by Bhag, Balwant and Rahim expressing solidarity with the passengers, men trooped to the front of the hall to cover a table with money and pledges. Many put down their entire savings, removing bills from pockets and from beneath turbans. Others pledged real estate titles. The largest donation was $2,000 in cash; the second largest, $1,000, came from a young Sikh on crutches: he had been injured in a saw-mill accident.

While the committee was raising funds on shore, Gurdit was preparing to deal a bold card—a starvation plea—to the white authorities. On June 4 he cabled a message to King George V in London and the Governor General in Ottawa:

"No provisions since four days. [Malcolm] Reid refuses supply charterer, and passengers starving; kept prisoners."

Neither His Majesty nor the Governor General, the Duke of Connaught, answered the cables. The King was too preoccupied gazing at the gathering war clouds to bother about a comparatively minor squabble in the far-off wilderness, and the Duke of Connaught, Queen Victoria's third son, probably considered it an unimportant bore.

But when Malcolm Reid learned of the messages, his response was quick in coming. In a lettergram to immigration superintendent Scott, he termed Gurdit's starvation claim "absurd." The immigration guards on board the freighter, he said, informed him that the Punjabis were secretly eating in the dead of night. Reid used the same lettergram to outline a proposal submitted by

Gurdit and Bird. Scott had bowed to Bird's demand for
a face-to-face conference with his client and a two-hour
parlay was held June 4.

But not on board the *Komagata Maru*. While adhering
to Scott's order that the two men should meet, Reid
stubbornly maintained that the lawyer must be banned
from the ship. The early-morning *tête-à-tête* therefore
took place in the harbor, 300 yards off the freighter's
stern: two government launches were anchored side by
side and the attorney talked to his client across two feet
of water. That afternoon Bird handed the inspector a
statement containing the conditions he and Gurdit had
drawn up. Reid told Scott:

"Bird asks submission following proposition. Gurdit
Singh will provide proper detention shed in which place
Hindus on shore and supply provisions while right of
Hindus to land is being determined. Will furnish immi-
gration department for return of all ordered deported.
Himself returning to India immediately on *Empress of
Russia* eleventh instant. This will allow him to sell cargo
Komagata Maru and take out cargo on her from here."

No sooner had he listed the Gurdit-Bird terms than
he set about advising Scott to reject them. If they
were accepted, Reid said, it could be "construed as
weakness on part of government," and "if these men
permitted on shore [there is] danger of riots by white
population." Moreover, he said, it would be "dangerous,
difficult and expensive to guard a large body of men for
lengthy period of time necessary to carry out involved
legal proceedings," and should Gurdit Singh journey to
India alone he "could cause trouble and influence the
Indian Government to place obstacles in way of this
department successfully ridding this country of this
shipload."

Reid's views won out; Scott rebuffed the Gurdit-Bird proposal 24 hours after receiving it.

The outright dismissal may have provoked the passengers' next move. Whatever the reason, they began harassing the shipboard guards. One immigration officer reported that several East Indians dangled him by his feet over the side of the boat until he passed out; another said five knife-wielding Sikhs surrounded him, saying they were famished and human testicles were an Asian delicacy.

When Reid heard the guards' complaints he thought about bringing in the militia and having armed soldiers patrol the decks. He decided against it, though, because such an iron-fisted maneuver might spark a riot aboard the ship and, instead, he withdrew his guards.

Gurdit Singh dispatched a pair of pleading messages to the Governor General on June 6 and 7. The first cable urged the appointment of a special commission to investigate Malcolm Reid's "cruel treatment" of the passengers. The second wire read:

"Reid disallowed my landing; have coal cargo to sell, can't take more cargo; suffering heavy [monetary] losses and starvation."

Was Reid starving the passengers? He certainly did not think so. Gurdit had been pestering him to send free food to the ship since the end of May. The Sikh leader's appeals came in written form: Reid visited the vessel regularly (he was processing Board of Inquiry applications) but he and Gurdit rarely talked to each other, a carry-over from their first stormy meeting. Gurdit's persistent pleas could not sway Reid. He was sure there was plenty of food hidden below deck—the guards had convinced him of that—and, anyway, he felt it was Gurdit's responsibility, not the Canadian government's, to feed the passengers.

In one respect, and only one, Reid and Gurdit were alike. Both were incredibly bull-headed. The *Komagata Maru* struggle was, in fact, essentially a contest between these two stubborn individuals. Neither wanted to yield an inch and when one of them did bend a little or was forced to completely back-pedal it must have been an exceptionally humiliating experience.

In any case, it was Reid who relented in the food quarrel: if Gurdit would pay the grocery bill, the Immigration Department would absorb the cost of picking up the provisions at the store and of having them delivered on the *Winimac.* The inspector was prompted to make the offer by a letter from the *Komagata Maru*'s resident physician, Dr. Raghunath Singh. A former British Army medical officer, Dr. Singh wrote Reid on June 8 declaring that a poor diet and a lack of medical supplies had several passengers rapping on death's door. Reid realized that if any of the Punjabis died while Gurdit was emitting starvation noises, his handling of the issue might be severely criticized by Scott and other Ottawa bigwigs.

The Immigration Department's medical expert, Dr. Monro, was sent to the freighter. His task was twofold: he was to apprise Dr. Singh that he could come ashore to purchase medicine if accompanied by an immigration guard and he was to convey Reid's offer to Gurdit. The government doctor was in the tiny cabin the physician shared with his wife and child when Gurdit burst into the room. He accused Dr. Singh of arranging some kind of underhanded deal with the Immigration Department. Could the Punjabi doctor be furnishing information about the passengers in exchange for landed immigrant status?

No, it could not be, Dr. Singh protested. He already had Canadian domicile, so why should he sell out his fellow countrymen when he would be admitted anyway? To be absolutely certain that the Board of Inquiry did not take a notion to deport him, domicile or not, Gurdit shot back.

Dr. Monro interceded on the physician's behalf. He explained about the medicine trip and he told Gurdit of Reid's food suggestion. Gurdit was far from elated. The Canadian government should be buying the provisions, he said, as it was Malcolm Reid's fault that the passengers were imprisoned on the ship. What was more, the expense Reid was willing to incur was paltry compared to the cost of the food.

But Gurdit accepted the compromise arrangement. If he did not, he said, people in high government offices could say he sneered at a friendly offer and he would be the culprit if an ailing passenger succumbed.

A wholesale grocer filled Gurdit's shopping order, the *Winimac* delivered the goods and Reid happily telegraphed Scott the news that the passengers were seen cooking a hearty meal at mid-deck.

Had the Punjabis really been starving or was it just a fable invented by Gurdit to badger the government? To this day, opinions differ: whites remembering the episode say Gurdit was lying; reminiscing East Indians say the absence of food nearly took several lives. Wherever the truth lies, both Gurdit and Reid profited from the incident. The *Komagata Maru* stayed on the front pages, causing governmental discomfort and thus giving Gurdit more bargaining clout in future negotiations. But it indirectly resulted in Reid's gaining an enlightening insight into the Rasputin-like power Gurdit had acquired over the passengers. That insight was provided by none other than the short, plump and middle-aged Dr. Singh.

Coming ashore to purchase medicine, an immigration guard in tow, the physician was approached on a waterfront street corner by Bela Singh, an East Indian working for the Immigration Department. Bela asked him to do what Gurdit mistakenly believed he was already doing—to tell Reid about shipboard activities. The doctor flatly refused.

Then, five days after the provisions were put aboard the ship, Dr. Singh penned a furtive note to Reid disclosing that Gurdit was persecuting him and he was worried about his personal safety. The note said:

"I beg to inform you that I am in great danger; the charterer and the passengers of this ship think me a secret spy . . . They have begun to abuse me on the face, which I cannot stand. I am in their hands and they might do the worst thing.

"The charterer does not wish me to remain in his service. Please take immediate action to avoid consequences. Give me a right to land or arrange my returning back to Hong Kong by another steamer. I am willing to pay the ship fare, etc., myself. Please do something or else I will be obligated to seek the protection of higher authorities."

Reid's reply read: "I regret there is any difficulty at all between your fellow passengers and yourself. Let me know at once if there is any sign of this coming to a head and I will do what lies in my power to give you the assistance necessary. I regret that owing to your name appearing on the Manifest as a passenger, I am prevented from dealing with your case any differently to the other passengers on the ship.

"The statements made by Gurdit Singh as to your being a detective are, of course, absurd. At the same time, knowing the fanaticism and credulous nature of many of your fellow passengers, I can quite understand how you are being annoyed; however, as I stated before, let me know at once if any contingency arises which demands immediate action and I will take such steps as will end your troubles."

The reserved tone of Reid's communiqué disguised his real feeling. With great delight he told an immigration colleague that Gurdit was foolishly pushing the physician into the government's waiting arms. He was right. On his next medicine trip, Dr. Singh consented to an interview with a West Coast Member of Parliament, H. H. Stevens.

The Conservative politician was keeping an eye on *Komagata Maru* developments for Prime Minister Borden, but his personal involvement went much deeper than that. He was a fervent exponent of nonwhite exclusion: he was not, of course, the only public figure railing against Asian immigration in pre-World War I British Columbia but he was the best-known and the most persistent.

Yet even his foes had to pay tribute to his honesty, doggedness and courage. A one-time mule skinner, locomotive fireman and prospector, the short, slimly built Stevens had burst into politics with giant-sized gumption. While working as a bookkeeper at a Vancouver grocery store in 1903, he discovered that two clerks were stealing money to cover losses racked up in gambling houses. A devout Methodist, he asked the police chief to crack down on the illegal establishments. The chief tossed him out of his office.

Concluding that the chief was in league with the gamblers, Stevens moved to end the cozy arrangement. He visited the gambling dens, then bought advertising space in a newspaper and published details of everything he had seen. The chief was fired and the dens padlocked.

Stevens later prodded the police into closing a string of brothels and banning the sale and smoking of opium on Chinatown streets. His reputation as a plucky crusader earned him a 29-year run in the House of Commons. And in a 1911 election victory speech, a 32-year-old Stevens gave this opinion on immigration:

"The immigrant from northern Europe is highly desirable, the immigrant from southern Europe is much less so, and the Asiatic, and I wish to emphasize this, is entirely undesirable."

Dr. Singh, of course, knew nothing of Stevens' exclusionist views when he agreed to an interview. Their meeting was set for Malcolm Reid's office on a Saturday afternoon at four o'clock. Reid and immigration officer William Hopkinson were also in attendance. So was a lady stenographer; thus the Stevens-Dr. Singh conversation was duly recorded:

"*Stevens:*   They are telling me that you are a little bit afraid of your personal safety.

"*Dr. Singh:*   Yes, I am afraid of my safety.

"*Stevens:*   Some of them threatened you did they?

"*Dr. Singh:*   Yes, Gurdit Singh threatened that they [the passengers] were going to kill me. Because I was allowed to come ashore and purchase medicine, they think I have spoken against them.

"*Stevens:*   Most of these men, doctor, are more or less ignorant are they, and don't understand the necessity of your coming ashore?

"*Dr. Singh:*   Yes, they are most of them and they do not understand. The real reason Gurdit Singh is against me is I have been telling the passengers what he has been doing to them. He did not deal with them properly.

"*Stevens:*   Is it correct Gurdit Singh rules the ship? Some of them [say], for instance, he puts them in irons.

"*Dr. Singh:* Oh, yes, quite true that he rules the ship. He puts a guard on anybody's room if he thinks they are against him. That is what he did to me. He put five or six men in front of my cabin and about five or six on top.

"*Stevens:* All the time did he put a guard? You weren't allowed to go up on deck?

"*Dr. Singh:* I was not permitted to . . .

"*Stevens:* About the men on board—they are not really the best of Hindu people are they? I know the Hindu people pretty well. I think a lot of them. Most of them on board appear to me to be pretty ordinary people—ordinary Hindus—you know, the ordinary working type.

"*Dr. Singh:* That I cannot say. Most of them served in the militia and they have left the service. Of the men who came from Shanghai and Hong Kong, practically all were working [in those places] in the police or as watchmen, things like that . . .

"*Stevens:* Are they kind of split up – two factions – some that are satisfied and some that are not?

"*Dr. Singh:* There are two men that are all right but on account of a large party being on the other side they cannot do anything. They are afraid to do anything.

"*Stevens:* Gurdit Singh has got some very strong control over their minds.

"*Dr. Singh:* I know that. If he was not on the ship there would be no trouble. Some of the men are his own men. He has promised to pay them something. I have no proof as to that but I think so. This statement you are taking . . .

"*Stevens:* This is made for myself and Mr. Borden. These local Hindus are sending out all manner of erroneous statements, you see, and they send these statements to Eastern Canada. I want to get before Mr. Borden as nearly as I can the facts, and you are kindly giving them to me, and I shall send them to him, you see. That is my whole object.

"*Dr. Singh:*   I don't want to make an enemy of the Indians in Vancouver.

"*Stevens:*   What is the condition of the men on board? Are they in fair health?

"*Dr. Singh:*   Some are getting bronchitis.

"*Stevens:*   Will it get serious?

"*Dr. Singh:*   I cannot say. One or two men have other trouble but the rest have bronchitis. They don't keep the ship sanitary. If a man has bronchitis, he spits all over the boat.

"*Stevens:*   Does Gurdit Singh make an effort to keep the ship clean?

"*Dr. Singh:*   I have told him many times to clean the ship and keep it clean. He says it is the work of the sailors, he is not going to do it. He does not think anybody has the authority to say anything to him. He has got his little island and he rules it.

"*Stevens:*   Does the Captain seem to be afraid of him?

"*Dr. Singh:*   He must be. He has a small crew and there are so many [passengers].

"*Stevens:*   Do you think they will go to the extent of fighting [if deported]?

"*Dr. Singh:*   They have not got anything to fight with. Nothing but clubs. They hold meetings every night. I was not allowed to go in there.

"*Stevens:*   Well, I think that is all I want to ask you today. Let me know, doctor, if there is anything I can do."

There was something Stevens could have done later on that day but Dr. Singh had no way of letting him know. Going back to the ship, he was seized by four Punjabis, roughed up and thrown into his cabin. The clandestine visit to the Immigration Building had delayed his return and Gurdit, his suspicions aroused, declared the physician would never get out of his cabin again. At least, not alive.

Four

DR. SINGH WAS still languishing in shipboard captivity as the *Komagata Maru* stalemate entered its third week. It was to be a week filled more with bombast than any major accomplishments. Two mass meetings, one organized by the East Indians on shore and the other by the whites, would only serve to heighten the tension in an already tense city.

The Board of Inquiry's lack of progress added to the general feeling that the *Komagata Maru* affair was far from over. For a while the board seemed headed for a quick resolution to the situation. It commenced by summoning the 22 passengers possessing Canadian domicile, hearing their stories and releasing them from custody. But when faced with the 90 Punjabis whom Dr. Monro deemed physically unfit the board lost its speed and, apparently, its nerve.

The immigration doctor recommended that the 90 be deported immediately because they posed a health hazard to the city. The board read his report, then sheepishly announced in mid-June that it was reserving its judgment.

Edward Bird did not think much of the board's impartiality—its five members, all immigration staffers, included Malcolm Reid. He thought even less of its do-nothing attitude regarding the sick passengers. The board was behaving scandalously, he protested in a letter to the immigration inspector. It was supposed to render a deportation edict or permit a landing; instead, he said, it was timidly avoiding a clear-cut verdict, perhaps trying to delay the court battle it might lose. According to Bird, the Board of Inquiry was a "travesty of justice" in which the "prosecutors are the judges."

In spite of the board's procrastination, the passengers were gaining a little ground on shore. The Temple Committee had collected enough cash by diligently following up on pledges to pay Bird's fee and to liquidate the charter debt. And the committee took a step that it felt would improve the passengers' relationship with the Immigration Department. Priest Bhag Singh and journalist Hoosain Rahim became the official charterers, signing a pact with Gardiner Johnson, a local shipping agent. The committee reasoned that Malcolm Reid might even let the *Komagata Maru* unload her coal cargo if he did not have to deal exclusively with Gurdit Singh.

Bhag, Rahim and Johnson formed an odd combination. A pillar of white society, the shipping agent was president of the Vancouver Cricket Club and a mainstay of the prestigious Union Club. Overcoming his poor beginnings in Scotland, Johnson had acquired, in his adopted country, the dignified no-nonsense bearing of a man born to wealth and power. Bhag and Rahim were considerably less correct and stately in their behavior.

Meanwhile the Vancouver press continued its attacks. In a pair of articles on June 18 and 19, the *Sun*'s Pollough Pogue ranted: "Right-thinking people know that the natives of Hindustan . . . should not be allowed in this country, except for circus purposes . . . We do not think as Orientals do. That is why the East Indians and other Asiatic races and the white race will always miscomprehend each other . . .

"[The Sikhs] are like the Irish raised to the nth or the fourth dimension. They are remorseless politicians and disturbers. They are complex and quite unaccountable . . . For the sake of the picturesque I am glad to have a few specimens. But those who came last [on the *Komagata Maru*] are not quite up to the sample. They must be returned as such."

The newspaper jibes infuriated the local Sikhs, and a mass rally was scheduled for the afternoon of June 21 at Dominion Hall, a spacious auditorium located at 337 West Pender. H. M. Fitzgerald, the Socialist Party of Canada's B.C. chieftain, was invited to address the rally. Fitzgerald's party had proclaimed in mid-June that it was throwing its somewhat skimpy weight behind "the beleaguered working men of Hindu extraction being oppressed by our ruling class-oriented government."

The rally had a festive flavor to it. Between speeches the 125 socialists in the hall waved red flags, clapped their hands in unison or shouted for the demolition of the capitalist system. Whenever their rowdy outbursts subsided, the 800 East Indians in attendance chanted hymns or listened reverently to musicians performing ragas on sitars and tablas.

The pudgy, beetle-browed Fitzgerald was a bit of a disappointment. His words were honey to the local East Indians backing the nationalist movement in India but, rather than buttressing the *Komagata Maru* cause, they detracted from it. Said Fitzgerald:

"Never mind Canada, there isn't very much in Canada. Also, never mind wasting your energies on the *Komagata Maru*. Get back to your own land filled with the spirit of revolt and sweep the country, and then fight the people that we socialists of North America are fighting . . .

"Go back and with your two hundred and sixteen million express the fighting power on your own behalf and, when you have expressed it, come again and so deepen the respect of the white man that no measly, no insignificant officer, will even attempt to stand on the gangway and prevent your landing . . .

"When I come to think of the revolutions made by the heroes of revolt in London, England, I feel like a man drawing near an insane asylum, and it is time you average people understood some of the outrages committed in India, compared to which the *Komagata Maru* is a mere farce . . .

"How the press can lie. I have nothing but pity for the individual who must work for the press. I would sooner die of starvation—I would sooner die of a dirty, foul disease—than be in the employ of the average newspaper."

Fitzgerald's speech elicited a lively ovation from his followers and the East Indian nationalists; the rest of the audience clapped more out of politeness than sympathy with his views. Edward Bird's speech, on the other hand, drew enthusiastic applause from everyone. The paunchy lawyer obviously did not share the saber-rattling socialists' opinion that neither Canada nor the *Komagata Maru* were worth bothering about. Bird told the gathering:

"I know my own people of a couple of centuries ago migrated to this country from Ireland because they were poor. They needed a change in a new land where land was free and where institutions were favorable to allowing their family to grow up and expand. Actuated by the same motives these people [the passengers] want to come to our country because there is not a country under the sun that is so glorious as our Canada."

For the most part, Bird's address was an up-to-date summary of *Komagata Maru* events. He triggered a thundering foot-stamping demonstration when he said the Immigration Department, the "most autocratic of our institutions," was managed by law-defying anarchists "who have told me they do not know if they'll abide by the Supreme Court orders if they let the passengers stay in Canada." It would be a strange spectacle, he said, should the provincial government have to pit troops against the immigration officers to enforce a court ruling.

Bird flayed the Board of Inquiry for postponing its sick-passenger decision and, he said, Dr. Monro's conclusion that trachoma was a disease deserving deportation was debatable.

"I know that men can live to old age with trachoma. There is some small substance in the eye, that's all. It is only contagious if people are careless with towels and so on."

Referring to Malcolm Reid and his staff as little Caesars, he spoke of the ban keeping him off the freighter and the Immigration Department's round-the-clock nautical patrol.

"I have been told that if I put my foot on the gangway an immigration officer will throw me in the ocean. I tell you, gentlemen, there is not a single thing from one cover of the Immigration Act to the other to authorize the immigration authorities to take possession of that ship illegally. They may go on board to conduct their normal duties but that does not authorize them to have an armed patrol."

The crowd dispersed quietly following the reading in English and Punjabi of a message Lal was cabling to Prime Minister Borden. The message read:

"We protest against the unlawful treatment given by the immigration authorities to the men on board the *Komagata Maru* in the harbor of Vancouver. These immigration people are so hard-hearted that they are going to practise any kind of brutality that they can lay hand on."

The rally and its aftermath—the *Sun* headlined its coverage, "Hindus Hold Mass Meeting and Preach Sedition and Treason"—spurred the white community into motion. A protest meeting was hastily organized for the next night at the same building. Mayor T. S. Baxter, Alderman Frank Woodside and ex-Liberal M.P. Ralph Smith would address the gathering, but the speaker expected to carry the ball most effectively for the whites was Conservative parliamentarian H. H. Stevens.

Five

WRITING IN THE February, 1912, edition of the *Monetary Times*, H. H. Stevens had stated precisely what he thought of the average East Indian:

"The Hindus will not assimilate but they will segregate in ill-ventilated and unsanitary surroundings, harboring disease and immorality. Their word is unreliable and this is so far established that many of our judges will not take their cases unsupported by white men . . .

"British Columbia is opposed to Asiatic immigration because it retards the development of the country and makes impossible a happy, permanent, intelligent people. It also results in a large alien male population with much immorality, where there should exist a community of white families . . ."

As Stevens' theories corresponded with those of the vast majority of B.C. workers, it was a piece of natural casting that placed him in the role of principal speaker at the protest meeting.

Given his reputation as an orator, it was natural too that Stevens' appearance would pull a fair-sized crowd, but the meeting organizers failed to anticipate the number of people that arrived. When the doors swung open at 7:45 P.M., 2,000 persons surged into the auditorium, filling all seats and occupying every foot of standing-room space. Several thousand more whites congregated outside the hall, staging an impromptu rally of their own with speakers dispensing rhetoric from the roofs of parked cars.

A small group of East Indians trying to get into the building after the rally started were jostled by the mob and chased down Pender street. The two dozen Punjabis already inside were also subjected to abuse. When Hoosain Rahim climbed to his feet and attempted to explain the passengers' side of the dispute to the crowd, a policeman flung him off the balcony.

Rahim was not seriously hurt and neither was H. M. Fitzgerald: standing near the front door, the socialist firebrand was punched and kicked repeatedly by a group of white laborers before police rescued him. Some East Indians had to endure coarse language and the odd shove, but the fact that most came armed with sturdy walking sticks helped keep the crowd at bay.

Mayor Baxter, a former lawyer and schoolteacher of United Empire Loyalist stock, took note of the audience's ugly disposition and, calling the meeting to order at eight o'clock, he urged the spectators to cool their tempers: violence, he warned, would weaken their case in the minds of the Ottawa power elite.

To loud applause, the mayor said Vancouver had all the workers it needed and the city opposed the importation of any laborers, whatever their nationality. Then he introduced Stevens. Donning a pair of pince-nez glasses, the Tory M.P. walked to center stage and eloquently, passionately, listed his objections to the *Komagata Maru* mission:

"What we face in British Columbia and in Canada today is this—whether or not the civilization which finds its highest exemplification in Anglo-Saxon British rule shall or shall not prevail in the Dominion of Canada. I am absolutely convinced that we cannot allow indiscriminate immigration from the Orient and hope to build up a nation in Canada on the foundations upon which we have commenced our national life. I hold that no immigration is or can be successful unless it is capable of being assimilated and absorbed by the people of the country to which it comes and without any detriment to that country . . .

"In the Orient, at our doors, there are eight hundred million Asiatics—and mark you I care not how high a value they place on their civilization—it is distinct in all its features from that which we hold dear. Eight hundred millions—the least tremor from that source would unquestionably swamp us by weight of numbers.

"Why, there is no people in existence that can absorb one, two, three, four, five times their number and I ask you this—what state would British Columbia be in today if Asian immigrants had been allowed through all these years to come through its portals? Canada would be swamped with Orientals and there would be left practically not a vestige of the civilization of which we are so proud."

Stevens scotched two rumors: he had not implored the government to tow the *Komagata Maru* out of the harbor and to cut it loose at mid-ocean, he said, and he had not requested an army brigade to protect Vancouverites from a Sikh uprising.

Stevens was roundly applauded when he mentioned the bill he had introduced at the last Commons session proposing the exclusion of all immigrants coming from Asia south to the 50th parallel. The bill was defeated but, he said, he planned to reintroduce it at an upcoming sitting.

The statement that detonated the evening's most prolonged blast of clapping, foot-stamping and cheering came near the end of Stevens' address. This was his criticism of the provincial judiciary:

"We have on the Bench of British Columbia today men who are willing to give a decision contrary to the general public opinion and contrary to what is the clear meaning of the Immigration Act. Some people say, why don't you go to the courts with your case? We are prepared to go to the courts if we can get a fair court to go to!"

Stevens was all but admitting the Board of Inquiry was purposely dragging its feet in order to delay a date in court. His admission revealed the difference of opinion existing within the government ranks. Prime Minister Borden and Robie Reid were still eager to settle the matter in a quick test case; Stevens and Malcolm Reid presumed such a procedure was too risky.

In his speech, Alderman Woodside, a former coal miner and union organizer, claimed British Columbia was "getting a bad name" in Great Britain because "our industries are full of Orientals." Ralph Smith, an

11-year Commons veteran, said he was concerned about Asian immigrants imposing their "degrading" living conditions on white Canadians.

A forest of sky-stretched hands passed a resolution put forward by Alderman Woodside imploring the federal government to immediately deport the *Komagata Maru* passengers and to bar all Asian immigrants henceforth. The only arms raised in opposition belonged to the East Indians and a small band of socialists. With this vote the crowd dispersed into the relative calm of the Vancouver night.

Did the mass meeting accomplish anything?

Stevens believed it did. In a 1973 interview, the 94-year-old ex-politician told me:

"Eastern Canadians were terribly ignorant about British Columbia and its problems. The Rocky Mountains, the broad Prairies, the contrasting life styles all tended to make B.C. seem like a semi-civilized hinterland to most Easterners. It was a Herculean task to interest eastern M.P.s in B.C. issues. They weren't just ignorant, they were indifferent too.

"Newspaper reports of the meeting showed Easterners how strongly the ordinary citizen objected to the *Komagata Maru*'s presence. The Woodside resolution, telegraphed to Mr. Borden and his Cabinet, showed them tersely and clearly what the B.C. working man wanted done with the ship."

Mayor H. C. Gray of neighboring New Westminster suggested another way in which the wall of eastern indifference could be battered down. He proposed at a city council meeting the following day that the passengers be transported to Ottawa in cattle boxcars so the government mandarins could see for themselves why British Columbians were so upset.

Six

IN THE AFTERMATH of the mass meetings, a scheme almost as bizarre as Mayor Gray's was regarded seriously within the corridors of power: it originated with the government's trusted West Coast lieutenants, Stevens and Malcolm Reid.

The two men hatched the idea of shanghaiing the *Komagata Maru* passengers and returning them to the Orient aboard a Canadian Pacific liner, the *Empress of India*. This was one of three *Empress* liners that went into operation in 1891, plying routes connecting

Vancouver with Hong Kong, Shanghai and Yokohama.
Scheduled to sail June 25, the graceful, twin-stacked
steamer could, they reasoned, pretend to be slipping out
to sea but, as she neared the freighter, she could
abruptly change course and pull alongside the *Komagata
Maru*. A contingent of policemen on the *Empress* would
spring from hiding, board the freighter and herd the
passengers onto the liner. Stevens and Reid reckoned
that Gurdit Singh and his horde would be so stunned by
the lightning-fast maneuver they would not have time to
put up a struggle.

On the evening of June 24, Reid wired the shanghai
proposal to Scott. The CP brass was considering a
charity rate, roughly $35 a passenger, and, he said, the
federal government would not have to pay more than
$15,000, including the salaries of special guards needed
to keep the peace during the voyage. He added that he
could hold the *Empress* in her berth a few hours beyond
her scheduled departure while awaiting Ottawa's answer.

Ottawa's answer crossed Reid's untidy desk the next
morning:

"Do not hold Empress. Wiring full instructions this
afternoon."

It was a glum Reid who got that message from Scott
and the one following it. Scott had spoken personally to
the Prime Minister and, he explained in the second telegram, the *Empress* plot was rejected on the grounds that
it might cause bloodshed.

Ottawa's dismissal of the *Empress* scheme once again
postponed the *Komagata Maru* finale. Yet even if they
had known they had escaped a surprise attack and
deportation, the passengers probably would not have
been deliriously happy. They were too concerned with
their newest worry to let anything outside of a sudden

granting of Canadian citizenship status lift their down-cast spirits. The ship's water supply was gone.

Gurdit Singh appealed to both the Governor General and Malcolm Reid for assistance. The telegram he sent the Duke of Connaught read:

"Many requests to Immigration Department for water but useless. Better to shoot than this miserable death."

The letter delivered to Reid's office was less dramatic in content. Signed by Gurdit's secretary, Daljit, it read: "I have the honor to inform you several times about supplying fresh water but have no answer about it. All men are drinking dirty, bad water, which has put them to sickness of bad cough and throat sore, but this bad water has been also finished."

Reid wrote back asserting that the ship's co-charterers, Bhag Singh and Hoosain Rahim, should provide the water. He said he had read the telegram meant for the Governor General and was holding onto it in case the passengers decided against sending it. Gurdit retorted that he wanted the wire dispatched at once. His faith in Reid at a low ebb, he asked the telegraph company to send him a copy as proof that it had been transmitted east.

Gardiner Johnson, the shipping agent, explained Reid's position on the water to Bhag and Rahim, who said they would gladly furnish the funds for that purpose—but they wanted to visit the vessel first. Upon hearing their request, the inspector issued an emphatic no. He had banned all visitors from the *Komagata Maru*, he said, and, even if the ban did not exist, he would never permit "agitators" like them to board her.

On June 23, the co-charterers had risen to the top of Reid's hate list, occupying positions slightly below those gained by Gurdit and Bird. That was the day they thumbed their noses at his off-limits decree and attempted to break through the security net surrounding the ship.

Bhag and Rahim had appeared at Pier A a few minutes past noon. Bird was already there, natty in a cream-toned cotton suit and a jaunty straw boater. Under a hot sun, the lawyer was arguing with Reid and a couple of immigration officers.

Thirteen East Indians accompanied the co-charterers. They had not come in a body to aid Bird; they had left a Temple prayer meeting intending to communicate with the passengers using the semaphore system. One of them carried two Union Jacks. Both he and his contact on the ship were British Army veterans and they could exchange messages pertaining to friends or relatives living in the city.

All were drawn into a semicircle around Reid and Bird. Cool as he looked in his summer outfit, the attorney was sizzling inside. His voice flared and his arms jerked up and down. Gurdit had summoned him to the vessel, he said, and it was about time Reid stopped defying the law and let him go on board.

Reid was stiff and reserved. Bird could not go on the boat, he said, but he could have a second consultation as before, Gurdit in one launch and Bird in another. That was not good enough, Bird told him. He wished to speak to his client where there was no danger of immigration personnel overhearing every word and reporting later to Reid.

Rahim and Bhag now waded into the quarrel. The inspector promptly advised them to remain silent or to leave the wharf. Rahim's temper exploded. Turning to Bird, he said he would take him to the *Komagata Maru*, the government and Reid be damned. The feverish adrenalin of peril swept over the men on the pier. Rahim was suggesting an act that could produce an ugly clash.

Bird hastily denounced the idea of forcing their way past the immigration launch. He said the passengers' cause would suffer a jarring setback if their attorney wound up in jail.

Although Bird's position must have taken some wind out of his sails, Rahim said he still hoped to board the freighter, if only to get the better of the "arrogant Mr. Reid." The upshot of the discussion was the decision to hire one of the boats anchored off the wharf and to streak for the *Komagata Maru.* Within minutes, the 15 East Indians were scrambling onto a small fishing craft.

They were emboldened by the realization that the *Winimac* was experiencing engine trouble. The launch bobbed on the choppy waves near the freighter's stern, the two guards on board performing haphazard surgery on her innards. But as the fishing boat started up, the *Winimac*'s gasoline-driven motor spat, then roared into life. The East Indians and their slow-chugging craft were less than halfway to their goal when the larger, faster launch slipped across their path, coming to an idling halt.

The fishing boat made an awkward bid to poke her bow around the *Winimac*'s stern but the launch smoothly backed up, cutting her off. Some of the Asians suggested ramming the launch or boarding her and throwing the guards into the Inlet. Both notions were instantly discarded. One guard brandished a rifle, the other wore a holstered revolver on his hip. Bhag and Rahim concluded that the possibility of someone's being slain was too steep a price to pay for the pleasure of giving Reid a psychological boot in the pants.

The fishing boat returned to her mooring.

Reid meanwhile had telephoned the police and a squad of blue-uniformed officers descended upon the East Indians when they touched shore. No arrests were made; Bhag and Rahim were simply warned against future sorties of a similar nature.

Small wonder that the co-charterers' promise to supply water once they visited the vessel elicited a blunt "no" from the inspector. Small wonder, too, that three days after Reid rejected their terms, Bhag and Rahim let their animosity for the inspector sway them into adopting a course of action that actually extended the passengers' suffering by keeping them without water.

Bhag and Rahim told Gardiner Johnson that the Temple Committee was destitute and it was now up to the city of Vancouver to donate free water under the Public Charges Act. The poverty plea was ridiculous. Had the committee really been penniless, the East Indian colony would have raised the money with the same expedition and generosity it had exhibited in amassing dollars to defray Bird's fee and the charter bill.

Nevertheless, Mayor Baxter was obliged to determine whether or not the passengers could qualify for civic charity. And while he was pondering the matter, cracks suddenly appeared in the solid front Gurdit Singh had been putting up on the freighter. The lack of water, the rapidly dwindling food stores, and the deep-seated misery caused by living in cramped, filth-ridden captivity had spawned a mutinous undercurrent in the ranks of the would-be immigrants.

A delegation of six or seven Sikhs, dubbing themselves the Komagata Maru Committee and purporting to represent one-quarter of the 354 passengers, approached the stocky leader with a pair of tough demands. First, they wanted to ascertain the whereabouts of some money Gurdit had gathered from the passengers for "safekeeping." Was it deposited in his Japanese bank account, as shipboard gossip had it, or was it on the boat where it could be spent on food and water? Second, they wanted Gurdit to go ahead with the test case. If the Board of Inquiry was so leery of the courts, perhaps they would get a favorable ruling after all.

True to his temperament, Gurdit responded angrily. He was in command of the expedition, he said, and he did not have to answer to a bunch of quivering upstarts. Nonetheless, he did answer. He swore he would hand over their money when they landed in Vancouver or Hong Kong, but he balked at disclosing where the funds were located. As for the test case, he said he had been thinking along the same lines and he had even come up with a suitable candidate—himself.

The committee voiced the theory that Gurdit was the worst candidate imaginable. The federal authorities despised him and they would tear him to shreds in court: the passengers' interests would best be served, the committee contended, if an unknown person was chosen.

Gurdit and the Komagata Maru Committee parted company with the test case question unsettled.

For two days the elder Sikh stayed in his cabin. If the committee did have the support of one-quarter of the Punjabis, it constituted a serious challenge to his leadership. Any hope of eliminating the dissension or at least stopping its spread most likely lay in his making a concession to the delegation. Whatever alternatives he considered, Gurdit terminated his two-day withdrawal by consenting to the test case and by helping the committee select a candidate other than himself.

Instead of one candidate, two were chosen, farmers Narain Singh and Munshi Singh. Gurdit and the committee agreed that Bird should interview both young men and pick the best one.

Upon receiving a letter from Gurdit notifying him of the test case approval, Bird conferred with Robie Reid and two other federal attorneys. All four lawyers concurred that the test case should be conducted under the conditions drawn up in May. A single passenger was to go before the Board of Inquiry and, if his entry application was denied, he could have access to the B.C. Court of Appeal. Should that august body rule against him, the entire *Komagata Maru* contingent would be deported.

Narain Singh and Munshi Singh were brought ashore and, after a thorough questioning alone with them at the Immigration Building, Bird chose Munshi.

Malcolm Reid made an 11th-hour bid to dodge the test case. In a lettergram to Scott, he urged the government to "use every means [to] avoid court procedure." Scott's reply, apparently dictated by the Prime Minister, said the board had the right to admit or deport the passengers but Reid was not to interfere at all should the Punjabis seek redress in court.

Munshi Singh faced the Board of Inquiry on June 28. Bird and his aide, Robert Cassidy, spoke for Munshi. He was a farmer, they argued, and could not be expelled under the Immigration Act clause barring foreign laborers and artisans. Furthermore, the "continuous journey" stipulation did not apply since Munshi was a British subject entitled to travel the Empire at will. The $200 the law said he had to have on his person? A relative on shore would give it to Munshi the moment it was needed.

Weary of the courts, but perhaps more weary of crossing swords with Borden, the board lost no time in passing judgment. That very afternoon it announced that Munshi was an illegal alien and must be deported posthaste. Bird and Cassidy packed their valises and took the next ferry to Victoria, the provincial capital.

Whatever verdict the five Appeal Court judges rendered, it would be a landmark, either curtailing future expeditions like the *Komagata Maru*'s or throwing the immigration floodgates wide open.

Seven

DAWN BROKE CLEAR and warm, the climbing sun spraying a butter-yellow veneer over the flags and banners hanging from lampposts and building façades. That traditional West Coast spoiler, gloomy, drizzling rain, had made itself scarce all summer and Dominion Day, 1914, was blessed with a cloudless sky.

The balmy weather assured a massive turnout for Canada's birthday celebration. Even the Court of Appeal had suspended its deliberation of the Munshi Singh case. By mid-morning Vancouver's most popular beach, English Bay, was a crazy quilt of multi-hued bathing suits. Men, women and children clustered near the busy diving board and giant wooden slide erected on a float 100 yards from shore. Where the water surrounding the float was not filled with swimmers, it was filled by holidayers in rented rowboats and canoes.

Stanley Park was mobbed, too, but the throngs streaming there were well distributed among 1,000 acres of trees, duck ponds, shaded trails and faithfully trimmed lawns and gardens. Lying between the city's heart and the entrance to Burrard Inlet, the sanctuary was still home to a smattering of native Indians, their ramshackle cedar huts the final remnants of the Salish enclave gradually phased out of the area since it became a park in 1889.

Few roads penetrated the region. The automobile was forsaken soon after driving over the stone-arched causeway spanning the tidal flat separating the park and the city proper. Dominion Day in Stanley Park was celebrated with family picnics, tennis and volleyball games and leisurely strolls amongst the stunning Douglas firs.

Across town, the Vancouver nine was playing Seattle in a baseball double-header at Athletic Park. Boxing, cricket and golf were also on the day's agenda, but the biggest slice of sporting hoopla was taking place at the Vancouver Ice Arena where promoter Con Jones was sponsoring a 12-hour Grand International Tug-o-War. Nineteen teams proudly displaying the emblems of different countries were competing for prizes totaling $1,600. The 72nd Highlanders Band, bagpipes skirling and drums pounding, paraded around the arena as nine-man teams sweated and strained their way through elimination matches. When the last muscle was flexed, John Devanay's Scottish squad emerged triumphant and received the $1,000 first prize from a beaming Mayor Baxter.

The exuberant atmosphere pervading the city was deceptive. On June 28 an assassin's bullet had killed the heir to the Austro-Hungarian throne, Archduke Ferdinand, and Europe was now precariously balanced on the rim of war.

The *Komagata Maru* seemed little more than a pesty fly in contrast to the elephantine crisis existing overseas. But whereas the citizens of Vancouver could only impotently observe the chilling theatrics being performed in the Balkans, they could at least have an active part in dispelling the comparatively insignificant menace lodged on their doorstep.

So once the flags and banners were put away, and once the populace resumed its nine-to-five devotion to commerce, the passengers came under attack again. Church, labor, civic and private organizations sent letters and petitions to newspaper and government offices urging the *Komagata Maru*'s expulsion, regardless of what the outcome of the Munshi Singh test case may be. Individual local citizens also took to the mails, and one of them, retired British Army officer Lieutenant-Colonel W. Ronaldson Clark, wrote B.C. Premier McBride:

"I hope I shall not see . . . in Victoria, four dirty *jat* [farmer] coolies squatting on the lawn in front of the Parliament Buildings and devouring an Indian meal out of a filthy piece of newspaper, as my wife saw last May when she was there. She said it was like the desecration of the beautiful gardens and that no one but an Indian would have the impertinence to do it."

The pen-wielding protesters might have been more sympathetic toward the passengers had they spent a day aboard the *Komagata Maru.* The Punjabis were now undergoing a severe food shortage. The supplies Gurdit had purchased in Vancouver were depleted and there could be no doubt this time that the stores bought in the Orient were all but exhausted.

The passengers were eating one meal a day and a lean one at that: it consisted primarily of potato soup and rice, prepared before the water supply ran out. On top of the food rationing, the July heat had the Punjabis thirstily contemplating the advisability of drinking the cool but salty sea water.

Unable or unwilling to make up his mind about providing fresh water, Mayor Baxter was given a second request to ponder: Gurdit wanted the city to donate a food shipment as well. Several passengers sought assistance from friends on Vancouver Island. Three main themes ran through their letters: (1) unless food and water was forthcoming, many people would die; (2) the Temple Committee had somehow gotten itself tangled in a mess of civic red tape; and (3) Gurdit Singh would not disclose the whereabouts of their "safekeeping" money.

The East Indian population on Vancouver Island was relatively small. But its members put long hours into back-breaking logging and mining jobs and they had abundant savings at their disposal. The letters of desperation prompted three Nanaimo Sikh leaders to travel to Vancouver, where they advised Malcolm Reid that the Islanders might put up the cash for provisions. In order to get an accurate picture of shipboard conditions, however, the trio felt a conversation with Gurdit and their distressed friends was essential. Could the inspector transfer these people ashore temporarily? Definitely not, Reid said. Gurdit was a crafty soul and he, Reid, would be roasted alive by his superiors if the old Sikh escaped and went underground in Vancouver.

Reid had an alternate proposition for them, though. The visitors could talk to whomever they wished from a government launch anchored hard against the freighter's leeward side. Of course, there was a disadvantage— immigration officers would hear everything they said— but it was the best he could do under the circumstances.

The Sikhs accepted. On Friday, July 3, at 11:30 A.M., the *Mary Ellen* set out from Pier A with the three Nanaimo East Indians and a fourth Sikh from Vancouver standing on her deck. Two immigration guards were on the launch and so was Harry Gwyther, an immigration officer fluent in the Punjabi language.

Reid was right in labeling Gurdit a crafty soul. Unfortunately, he did not understand just how clever he actually was. The former contractor was capable of transforming almost any contact with the authorities into a powder keg and the Nanaimo Sikhs' visit gave him ample material to work with.

As the launch dropped anchor beside the freighter, hundreds of passengers flocked to the railing, conversing loudly amongst themselves. The babble made it impossible for the Nanaimo Sikhs to be heard up on the *Komagata Maru* deck. Gwyther had been ordered not to allow the visitors on board the ship. But what about bringing a few passengers onto the launch? the Nanaimo delegates inquired. Surely, nothing could go awry if Gwyther limited their number to five or six?

In a written report to Reid, chief interpreter William Hopkinson recounted what occurred when Gwyther consented:

"Five Hindus, friends of those on the launch, came down the gangway to talk with those on our [the government's] boat. Shortly after these men put foot on the boat Gurdit Singh and his secretary instructed the passengers to pull up the gangway, thus leaving the five men on our boat. Mr. Gwyther remonstrated but his objections were to no avail. On his return to shore the matter was reported to me and I proceeded on board and talked the situation over with Gurdit Singh.

"Gurdit Singh informed me that these five men were in conspiracy with the Immigration Department and that the passengers would not permit their return on board. From my observation, I understood the whole affair is a plot on the part of Gurdit Singh and Daljit Singh, who have incited the passengers to this action with a view of causing inconvenience to the department . . ."

The stranded passengers had descended the gangway Friday at noon. They remained aboard the *Mary Ellen* all day, sitting on the deck, and were shifted to the roomier *Winimac* in the evening. The *Winimac* was short on sleeping accommodations, even though the four visitors and Gwyther had departed, and the five spent the night on the wheelhouse floor while the immigration guards occupied the bunks.

Reid summoned Captain Yamamoto, the freighter's chubby, moon-faced master, to his office Saturday, July 4. It was 10 A.M.; the five Punjabis had been off the freighter for 22 hours. The inspector declared that force would be employed if they could not be placed back on the ship by peaceful means. Two interpreters, William Hopkinson and a Japanese linguist named Yoshi, and a stenographer were in the office with Reid and the captain. The conversation opened with the skipper explaining he had been ashore since Friday. Reid then said he had gone to the vessel in the Captain's absence, accompanied by the ship's Japanese steward. Here is what followed (with Yoshi serving as translator):

"*Reid:*   We went out without you and spoke to your officer in charge requesting him to lower the gangway and take these men back on the ship. He was either unable or refused to lower it, although he was successful in placing a rope ladder for the steward to go on board. The Hindus would not permit the gangway to be lowered and said they would kill those men or any of our officers who came on board. I am going to ask you to go with us now. The captain is responsible. The men are passengers on his ship and must go aboard. Explain this to him, Yoshi.

"*Yoshi:*   He says he did his best to pacify the Hindus but they were very excited and his men and himself could not take the five Hindus on the boat now. He says he may be able to sometime after today but in the meantime his men are only a few and cannot resist all the Hindus.

"*Reid:*   Does the captain admit he cannot control his ship?

"*Yoshi:*   He says so far he could not control it.

"*Reid:*   Is the captain aware that Gurdit Singh is not the charterer and has nothing to do with the ship now?

"*Yoshi:*   He knows all about it but he tried his best to pacify Gurdit Singh but Gurdit Singh has no common sense.

"*Reid:*   Does the captain admit that when the time comes [to deport the passengers] he cannot control his ship?

"*Yoshi:*   Gurdit Singh told him if he was notified about rejection or refused the landing by your authorities, he is going back to the Far East.

"*Reid:*   Then he cannot state definitely that he is out of control of his ship?

"*Yoshi:* He thinks the Hindus are going back because they are packing their articles to go back. He [Gurdit] will have to pay more charter money if he stays until August.

"*Reid:* Those five will have to go on the ship. We will go with him to the Japanese consul and the chief of police. Let him tell the chief of police he must have help. We order them back; he is responsible for his ship. The police will go out; he must muster his crew and put the men on by force.

"*Hopkinson:* (to Yoshi) We will let you go on the *Komagata Maru* and explain this to Gurdit Singh. The second thing is Gurdit Singh has no command of the boat. The commander is the captain. When the captain says the gangway is to be put down, anybody who interferes is obstructing the commander. Tell Gurdit Singh he is doing wrong and that the captain is going to consult the chief of police and the Japanese consul, independent of the Immigration Department; that this is not a matter for the Immigration Department; that he will take action himself.

"*Yoshi:* He [Yamamoto] says Gurdit Singh sometimes looks like he is out of his mind a little bit. The captain says if he is given time, say a day, he may be able to arrange it [to get the five on board]. He says when he is on duty he can control the ship.

"*Hopkinson:* (to Yoshi) We will give him until Monday morning. When they are in port and can do this, what are they likely to do on the high seas? What guarantee have we that they will not beach the ship, say on the west coast of Vancouver Island?

"*Yoshi:* He says in case Gurdit tried to compel him to go someplace on our coast, there might be international trouble and the boat belongs to Japan, and he will do his best to go straight home. He believes that will not happen.

"*Reid:*   What about the situation today and his practical admission that he is powerless?

"*Yoshi:*   He says that is quite different.

"*Reid:*   We are not going to allow any provisions on board or any interviews to take place because they threatened our men. By Gurdit Singh's action, everything has ceased. He [Yamamoto] can have until Monday. If in the meantime Gurdit Singh is willing to allow the gangway to be let down, all he has to do is signal the boat and those men will go on board."

The manner in which Reid and Hopkinson manipulated Captain Yamamoto is intriguing. Bluntly, arbitrarily, the skipper was told what moves he was expected to sanction; if those moves encompassed police enforcement, the responsibility would be his and not that of the government agents pulling the strings. Another interesting aspect of the discussion was Captain Yamamoto's dread of bucking Gurdit Singh. When he discovered Reid was on the verge of calling in the constables, he attempted to alter the inspector's conception of his position on the ship. He had begun the conversation saying he was not in control; he ended it saying he would have control when he was on duty again.

Also apparent was the fact that Hopkinson was more than just an interpreter. He and Stevens were Reid's closest advisers and of the two Hopkinson was perhaps the more influential due to his background.

A lanky, narrow-shouldered, swarthy-complexioned man of 37, Hopkinson was the product of a mixed marriage between a British soldier and an East Indian woman. Raised in the Punjab, he harbored, it was said, a flaming hatred of all anti-English revolutionaries because his father was slain by a seditionist in 1878. In any event, he was a sepoy in the India Volunteer Rifles and an inspector with the Calcutta police prior to becoming police chief of Lahore and, in the latter post, a veritable plague on the houses of rebellious nationalists.

His diligent tracking and prosecution of seditionists was brought to the Canadian government's attention when some notorious radicals migrated to British Columbia and started turning out India-bound bombs and anti-British literature. In 1909 Hopkinson, a fellow so unassuming in appearance that you would never notice him in a crowd, was hired by the Immigration Department to help stem the rebel tide in Canada.

Hopkinson was entrusted with the day-to-day running of the small-scale spy ring the department operated in B.C. The ring exposed illegal East Indian immigrants, many of whom had slipped across the U.S.-Canadian border; and, by infiltrating rebel organizations, it zeroed in on bomb factories and printing presses.

The Japanese translator, Yoshi, belonged to the undercover network but in a minor capacity. His assignment during the *Komagata Maru* affair was to trail Captain Yamamoto whenever he came ashore. Yoshi's secret vigilance produced a report concerning the master's activities following his talk with Reid and Hopkinson.

After picking up a note from Hoosain Rahim in Chinatown, the captain had lunch with the Japanese consul, Hori. Yoshi slipped into an adjoining booth and overheard Captain Yamamoto state he had lost control of the ship. The two men spotted Yoshi and invited him to join them. During the meal Yoshi learned the Rahim note—a message saying the city still had not relented on the water issue—was meant for Gurdit Singh. The interpreter made Captain Yamamoto promise that

Malcolm Reid would see any future messages before he delivered them to the ship.

Upon leaving the restaurant, Captain Yamamoto and Hori walked to Gardiner Johnson's office. It is safe to speculate that the topic Johnson and Captain Yamamoto discussed that Saturday afternoon was the skipper's anxiety over police involvement, for that was the subject that dominated the proceedings when the two men met Reid and Hopkinson Monday morning at the Immigration Building. Seventy hours had passed since the five passengers became stranded, and Reid pressed the captain to round up his 35 crewmen and to assist the police in placing them back on the freighter.

The shipping agent said Captain Yamamoto did not feel any maritime law had been broken and he was sure a fight would break out if the lawmen appeared. Reid countered that the Immigration Department's lawyers stated the five must go on board, forcibly or otherwise.

Again speaking for Captain Yamamoto, Johnson said the captain felt he was obligated to take orders from Gurdit Singh. Reid and Hopkinson stressed that Bhag Singh and Hoosain Rahim were the charterers and Gurdit had no authority to give the captain orders. Be that as it may, Johnson said, the captain could not be dissuaded; to him, Gurdit was on equal footing with Bhag and Rahim, regardless of any official document.

The inspector closed the discussion on a threatening note. He might have difficulty restraining the white citizenry from manning tugs and towing the *Komagata Maru* out of port, he said, but he would give Captain Yamamoto until 6 P.M. to settle the squabble peacefully. If he could not do so, police action would be necessary.

Captain Yamamoto returned to the ship. The hours whittled down and the deadline lapsed without a discernible change in Gurdit Singh's stance. At 6:10, Reid had the *Winimac* deliver this letter to the captain:

"There are five men, passengers by the *Komagata Maru*, who have not been landed, who were allowed off the steamer for the purpose of conversation with friends but who have not been allowed to return to the steamer. Unless you permit these men to be put on board the *Komagata Maru*, we must take it that you are assisting them to land, or attempting to land them, which is against the provisions of the Immigration Act. Kindly therefore make arrangements to have these men put back on the *Komagata Maru* at once."

Two more hours passed and neither Captain Yamamoto nor Gurdit Singh made an effort to retrieve the five passengers. Reid, Gwyther and immigration officer Paul Howard steered the quintet onto the *Mary Ellen* and, with rifle-toting guards standing by on the *Winimac*, they rode the boat out to the *Komagata Maru*. Behind them, a solitary policeman was poised on Pier A, ready to summon additional constables should trouble develop.

Malcolm Reid wrote later: "The gangway was lowered and Gurdit Singh and his secretary came down, wishing to argue the point as to whether or not they would receive the five men back on board. I gave them two minutes in which to make up their minds, and ordered the rope thrown off. They then acquiesced and the five men went on board peaceably, avoiding possible complications which [immigration] officials have endeavored in every possible way to avoid."

There was another factor besides Reid's stern, unyielding front that led to Gurdit's capitulation. That was the verdict in the Munshi Singh case. Shortly before the *Mary Ellen* ferried the five passengers to the ship, Bird

wired the expedition leader the distressing news that the
five judges had voted unanimously to uphold the Board
of Inquiry ruling. The floodgates were sealed shut;
Canada would remain a white man's country.

Thus the 80-hour cliff-hanger ended in a tame climax.
To engage in a bloody scrap would have been a pointless
act. All hope for the passengers' admission had to be
scuttled; the Immigration Department was victorious
and, dejected and embittered, Gurdit Singh and his
flock were now priming themselves for a mortifying
voyage home.

Eight

THE SHIP STAYED in port. The passengers
could prepare themselves psychologically for the long
trip back to Hong Kong, but they had no way to prepare for their physical needs. And how could they cross
the Pacific without food and water?

Mayor Baxter had finally shown his hand—the city
would not donate a single crumb of bread nor a cup
of water to the Punjabis—and the federal government
and the co-charterers refused to foot the bill. (The
Nanaimo Sikhs dropped out of the picture, agreeing

to let the Vancouver colony resolve the predicament.

Besides their grudge against Malcolm Reid, the elderly, gray-bearded Bhag and the thirtyish, slender-bodied Rahim now had another reason for not supplying the provisions. They wanted to delay the freighter's departure because they were sowing the seeds of a daring conspiracy. Angered and depressed by the Munshi Singh decision, the two men decided to ask extremists belonging to the outlawed *Ghadr* party to help the passengers land.

The *Ghadr* (a word meaning "revolution" or "mutiny") had begun spreading its tentacles throughout British Columbia, California, Washington and Oregon around the turn of the century. Its avowed target was to drive the British from India by guerrilla warfare tactics, and the racial slurs East Indian immigrants encountered made the West Coast receptive ground for enlisting terrorist recruits.

On November 1, 1913, the party had launched a weekly paper, *Ghadr*, in San Francisco. The maiden issue carried an editorial summing up the party's *raison d'être*:

"What is our name? Ghadr. What is our work? Ghadr. Where will Ghadr break out? In India. The time will soon come when rifles and blood will take the place of pen and ink."

The paper gained a wide circulation amongst Canada's East Indian settlers, and Ghadrites often rose at Sikh Temple meetings to quote inflammatory prose from its pages. (In August, 1914, thousands of East Indians started sailing home from all over the world to participate in a Ghadrite uprising. Mahatma Gandhi and B. G. Tilak publicly scorned the party's violent methods and the terrorists failed to rally the general populace to its banner. The Ghadrites killed two people, a policeman

and a village bureaucrat, and the British crushed the
rebellion nine months after it began. The party itself
limped on in North America until the 1930s.)

Bhag was a greater devotee of the party's blood-and-
thunder dogma than Rahim was: the priest was one of
the individuals known to read the *Ghadr* aloud at
Temple gatherings. Rahim, whose monthly journal
mirrored his socialist beliefs, opined that the problems
aggravating East Indians in Canada should be put ahead
of those prevailing in their homeland, but he was a
Ghadrite supporter all the same.

Between these two, an astonishing offensive was
contrived. The co-charterers would balk at supplying
any provisions, and the passengers' hunger woes would
be front-paged on a global basis, causing an international incident and embarrassing the Canadian and
British governments.

The second phase of the plan involved a mass
escape. With a handful of guns the passengers could
overpower their guards and flee into the city. Local
East Indians would hide the escapees in their houses
or in the thick bushland to the north. The co-
charterers wanted the passengers transferred to the CPR
detention shed near Pier A to facilitate their flight. And,
because B.C. storekeepers would not sell weapons to
Asians, the guns the Ghadrites planned to smuggle to
the passengers would be obtained in Washington State
border towns.

The Ghadrites' intrigue was kept secret from the co-
charterers' lawyer. Bird believed too strongly in the
necessity of balancing right and wrong on the scales of
justice, in a dignified courtroom setting, to be trusted
by them. But he did have an inkling that Rahim and
Bhag had an underlying reason for not feeding the

passengers and, writing to Robie Reid on July 9, he indicated what that motive could be:

"I feel it will serve the purpose of the enemies of the Canadian and Indian governments if [the passengers] are to suffer further and any injury comes to them from the privations they are now suffering."

Bird held Robie Reid in high esteem, both as a person and as an attorney. That lofty opinion had risen even higher two days previously when the government counsel gained Malcolm Reid's promise to let Bird confer with Gurdit Singh aboard the *Komagata Maru*.

However, it was probably not Robie Reid's persuasive powers that achieved this but rather the inspector's notion that Bird's effectiveness had ended. Gurdit had contended all along that Reid really did not think the lawyer would smuggle guns on board; he had been banned from the ship to weaken his efforts on the passengers' behalf. It was after the Court of Appeal verdict was announced that Reid lifted the ban.

At any rate, Bird was at last able to speak to his client without a government audience and the pair spent over an hour in the Sikh leader's cabin. When he emerged, Bird possessed a single-paged document signed by Gurdit and six members of the Komagata Maru Committee.

Unaware of the Ghadrite escape plan, Gurdit and the committee had decided to waive future Board of Inquiry hearings—which in light of the Munshi Singh ruling were useless formalities—and to have Bird arrange for their swift return to Hong Kong. At the bottom of the document was a sentence stating that one passenger disagreed. The dissenter was the ship's medical officer, Dr. Singh: he said he had Canadian domicile and was entitled to land.

The next morning, having read the document, Malcolm Reid sent immigration officer Harry Gwyther to the ship to question the doctor. The interpreter's written statement said:

"He [Dr. Singh] informed me the passengers were mad at him for wanting a Board of Inquiry when they themselves had waived the right to one. He told me that while attempting to come to the gangway to speak to the patrol boat, he had been forcibly caught hold of and returned to his cabin; also that his sword, which he had with him, had been confiscated by them."

Dr. Singh was punished for eluding his guards and trying to signal the launch. Gurdit doubled the guard on his quarters. When the physician complained, Gurdit handed him the price of a second-class fare on the *Empress of Japan*, saying he would be placed on the liner when it sailed that week.

Daljit Singh spoke to Gwyther after he left the doctor's cabin. The secretary said Gurdit had given him the fare in a fit of anger and Dr. Singh would be permitted on deck if he gave it back. Dr. Singh did so but he and his family remained incarcerated, their apprehension growing daily.

On July 8 the passengers took a wild, last-minute swing at gaining entry. A telegram was dispatched to Ottawa requesting a tract of land in Alberta that they could communally cultivate. They were wasting their energy. The federal government was not apt to waver in its support of the Court of Appeal deportation edict. Not only that: the people of Alberta did not envisage nonwhite immigrants as God's chosen races either. Like B.C. the press in the Prairie provinces fanned the flames of racial strife, a fact well illustrated by a description of Vancouver's Chinatown printed in the *Edmonton Journal* on September 21, 1907:

"Let not the sympathy of the tender-hearted be aroused by these poor Chinks. They do not live like rats from force of circumstance. They prefer the stench and filth of their vile surroundings."

The land overture failing, the passengers renewed their pleas for food and water, swearing they would quit the harbor when sufficient supplies were stored in the hold. The Komagata Maru Committee wrote three letters to Malcolm Reid. Dated July 9, the third missive said the Asians had not eaten for three days and mentioned that the inspector had not replied to their first two hunger messages.

Reid did not answer because he had decided to talk to Gurdit Singh and the committee in person. On the afternoon of July 9, Reid went to the *Komagata Maru* to judge for himself the seriousness of the situation. He had not been on the ship for over four weeks. Realizing the Punjabis considered him their worst enemy, he had seen no point in boarding the ship if his presence would only cause more aggravation. But now the possibility that some of the passengers might actually be starving did, he felt, necessitate a personal visit.

Obviously, Reid could not fathom the depth of the Punjabis' hatred for him. To them, he was an arch-villain, the very essence of treachery and cruelty, a heartless beast who would push them starving into their graves rather than sanction their admission to Canada.

Had he known how thoroughly they despised him, the inspector might have taken a legion of bodyguards along. Accompanying him were only Hopkinson, Robie Reid's associate, W. H. D. Ladner, Bird's aide, F. D. Pratt, two young stenographers, and the *Sun*'s stellar example of a rotten reporter, Pollogue Pogue.

Not expecting visitors, Gurdit hurried off to his cabin the moment they appeared at the gangway. His squat frame was draped in white cotton trousers, worn at the knees, and a wrinkled white cotton shirt; such shoddy garb was, he deemed, unsatisfactory for a consultation with the smartly attired boarding party.

Five Komagata Maru Committee delegates—Amar Singh, Sundar Singh, Vir Singh and two persons named Hernam Singh—guided the visitors to an empty saloon that was blissfully remote from the rancid garbage heaped on the deck. Port regulations forbade the dumping of refuse in the Inlet and, with the summer heat pressing on it, the garbage had acquired a nauseating stench. (The smell was so putrid a stenographer fainted while crossing the deck. Contrary to immigration rules, one of the white males had a flask in his hip pocket and a generous dose of brandy revived the girl.)

Like Gurdit Singh, the committee members and most of the passengers had packed their best suits away; unlike Gurdit, no one else cared what the visitors thought of their white, pajama-style outfits and none of them dashed off for a quick change.

Why Reid brought two stenographers to the ship is puzzling. But it turned out to be a wise move; while the fainting girl monopolized an open porthole in the saloon, the other scribbled notes. The meeting started with the committee representatives declaring they had stripped Gurdit Singh of his powers and were now running the ship themselves. With Hopkinson translating, the discussion then lunged into a danger zone:

"*Hopkinson:* (to Reid) They state if food and water are not on board by nine o'clock, the passengers will rush the boats, taking the matter out of the hands of the committee, and go onshore. The passengers have told them this. Hernam Singh states that here is an opportunity for you to search the vessel and find out whether they have provisions or water.

"*Reid:* It is not necessary. I have already interviewed the mayor. He will try and fix the matter as soon as possible. If possible, tonight. [Mayor Baxter had made no such commitment.]

"*Hopkinson:* They want to know what the mayor said.

"*A Punjabi:* We are starving. If a continuation of consultations goes on, we are likely to be starving [to death] by the time action is taken.

"*Reid:* If we cannot fix it tonight, we will let them know and have it fixed tomorrow morning. Mr. Bird may have arranged it by now. Mr. Bird would have been here with us but he is working on this.

"*Hopkinson:* They say there are women and children on board. Starving. They say they can possibly do without provisions but they cannot do without water.

"*Reid:* It takes time to pump water in but we will hurry and try to fix this matter up.

"*Hopkinson:* They want a time within which this will happen.

"*Reid:* We will do our best tonight but the hour is late. If we can get the manager of the water works, it will be all right. How much water do they want until tomorrow? We can get that at once.

"*Amar Singh:* (to Reid) I would like you to be in the same position as we have been in and see how you feel about it individually, and what must be the case of men collectively in this respect. You are getting your food three times a day, and your water, and we are getting nothing. If you were starving for three or four days, you would soon take action to get something for yourself. We have addressed letters to you and complaints regarding several matters. We have made inquiries for you to your officers that come to this boat and they

Above: The Japanese freighter *Komagata Maru* at anchor in Vancouver harbor.

Below: Conditions were scarcely ideal for the 376 East Indians living aboard the freighter.

Above: Gurdit Singh and his son Balwant.

Below: left to right: Inspector Malcolm Reid; the Hon. H. H. Stevens, M.P.; and the Hon. Martin Burrell, M.P.

Above: From a poster of Mewa Singh: "A Sikh Martyr of Canada." (Sikh Temple, Vancouver, B.C.)

Below: The militia was called out to prevent a riot on Pier A before the *Komagata Maru* sailed.

Above: The cruiser HMCS *Rainbow*, called to aid in deporting the East Indians on board the freighter.

Below: The *Komagata Maru* being escorted out to sea by HMCS *Rainbow*. (Provincial Archives, Victoria, B.C.)

have always said, 'Mr. Reid is attending to this matter,' or, 'I do not know.' Now that you are here we would like to hold you until such time as your promise to send provisions and water is fulfilled.

"*Hopkinson:* (to white males) Matters are assuming a serious aspect. It is advisable that no demonstration on our part be made to resent the threat conveyed. Leave the matter in my hands. Get the stenographers out of the room and onto our launch."

Reid and the others stepped quickly to the door and, before another word was uttered, passed through it onto the deck. Hopkinson tried stalling the Punjabis, pretending to require details of the provisions they wanted. Ignoring him, the five men trailed the visitors outside.

Amar Singh shouted to the hundred or so Asians within hearing range that Reid should be stopped and held hostage. The crowd closed in, fashioning a circle of obdurate flesh. The whites were caught, unable to proceed in any direction.

Hopkinson entreated the passengers to be calm and not to block the boarding party's route to the gangway. They scoffed at him. Then a new voice rose above the exchange between the interpreter and the passengers—the voice of Dr. Singh. His face against the wheelhouse window, the doctor yelled that he was locked in there so Reid would not find him if he went to his cabin. The passengers were going to kill him, he said, and, the Immigration Department must provide protection.

With impeccable timing, Gurdit Singh loomed out of the mob, a commanding figure in a khaki suit, fresh white shirt and green tie. A nervous Captain Yamamoto was at his side. Fastening a rigid gaze on the captain, Reid ordered him to release and protect Dr.

Singh. If the physician was injured or slain, he said, the captain could be charged with aiding and abetting a criminal deed. Captain Yamamoto swore he would muster his crew later and free the doctor; it was an oath he never kept.

The inspector then said the captain was obligated to protect everyone on his ship—especially people in the employ of His Majesty's government. Captain Yamamoto's muttered retort went unheard.

Amar Singh continued to provoke the crowd. Maybe they should not bother holding Reid hostage, he shouted. Maybe they should kill him. The Asians responded instantly; knives, swords and clubs appeared in their hands. All of their hate, all of their frustration, was ready to explode in a frenzied spurt ridding them of their demon antagonist.

Not once in his dealings with the East Indians on the ship and on shore had Reid shown even the slightest glimmer of anxiety. The tall, square-jawed inspector always personified manly self-assurance and tenacity. Now, trapped and defenseless, his stony exterior crumbled. His handsome face pale, his voice uncertain, he admonished the passengers to lay aside their weapons. Murdering him, he said, would bring them more grief, incurring the redoubtable wrath of an avenging Canadian government.

The passengers mocked him. What would the government do—hang all of them? Then the one man the Punjabis would not ridicule, Gurdit Singh, surprised everyone by picking up Reid's cautioning theme. In advising the passengers to release Reid and the others, the older Sikh blatantly contradicted Amar Singh's cries for action. Gurdit won out; the passengers downed their weapons. It was, as it had never ceased to be, Gurdit Singh's ship.

The white males shouldered a path through the crowd to the gangway, the trembling stenographers sticking close to them. Descending to the *Winimac*, the boarding party saw a police patrol boat speeding toward the shoreline. The boat had neared the *Komagata Maru* at the height of the tense confrontation and had been driven off by passengers hurling stinking vegetables and fruit.

An argument erupted on the freighter as the visitors headed back to Pier A. The committee berated Gurdit for spoiling their hostage scheme. When the squabble ended, the committee went away reassured that it was calling the shots. Gurdit had outflanked the delegates by approving another concession: if Reid did not supply food and water, the passengers would storm the city in lifeboats.

Pollogue Pogue's version of the hostage episode was a collage of fact and fabrication. In a front-page article on July 10 the *Sun* reporter said that when Reid and Hopkinson boarded the vessel on a routine Board of Inquiry errand, the Asians threatened to hold the inspector captive but "the coolness of the white men assuaged the turmoil."

There was no reference to the other members of Reid's party; nor was there a solitary sentence about the meeting with the Komagata Maru Committee. On the credit side of the ledger, the *Sun* did publish a letter the committee wrote to Bird bemoaning the passengers' excessive hunger pangs, and there was Pogue's eyewitness testimony that "there is nothing aboard the ship for the Hindus to eat."

Gurdit Singh's unexpected peace-maker move was left out of the story and, alas, Reid neglected to mention it when he wrote Scott, perhaps leery of depicting himself in a situation he could not dominate.

So it was up to an ancient and remarkably durable form of communication, malicious gossip, to distribute the real story helter-skelter throughout the city. For days afterward, busy tongues passed on the amazing news that Reid probably owed his life to his principal adversary, the canny, unpredictable Gurdit Singh.

Nine

QUITE PLAINLY, THE white residents of Vancouver were all but aching to witness the last act in the *Komagata Maru* drama; so were the passengers, the Ghadrites and the government officials. The freighter had been in port nearly seven weeks. A deportation sentence had been pronounced and yet her fate was still unclear—the ship still seemed a floating, ticking bomb.

Malcolm Reid almost single-handedly bore the weight of public pressure demanding that the Immigration Department administer an adroit *coup de grâce* to the hapless voyagers. Adding immeasurably to that burden was the urgent necessity of preventing the passengers from raiding the city in quest of food and water. Although he had an aversion for compromise, the inspector knew that someone had to give in somewhere along the line and, he concluded, the most logical someone was T. S. Baxter, the diminutive, walrus-mustachioed ex-teacher serving his one and only term in the mayoralty seat.

When the *Winimac* docked following the anxious encounter on the freighter, Reid left Hopkinson and the other members of the boarding party and traveled directly to City Hall.

The mayor saw him the moment he arrived. The inspector told him of the invasion threat and asked the chief magistrate to change his mind about providing food. Impossible, Mayor Baxter asserted. The civic treasury could scarcely tolerate the strain of feeding poor whites, let alone a horde of undesirable foreigners.

The prospect of a Punjabi invasion failed to perturb the mayor. The police and the army could readily repel them, he said confidently. While the idea of pitched combat in downtown streets did not upset Mayor Baxter, it had Reid in a dither. From Prime Minister Borden on down, the reaction would be unanimous: who was responsible for letting things develop to the stage where lawmen and soldiers had to defend the city against a swarm of half-starved aliens? The newspaper editorialists would seek a scapegoat and, in all likelihood, that scapegoat would be Inspector Malcolm Reid. Clearly, the handsome Scot was skating on the thinnest of thin ice.

In 1973, Stevens recalled Reid's quandary and how he wriggled out of it: "Malcolm Reid was a model civil servant—loyal, tireless, adept at administrative budgets, and so forth. But his background had equipped him for duties in a relatively small city. He was not a big-leaguer, a chap born to be in the throes of a crisis with international complications.

"He depended on Ottawa and his close associates for guidance in the *Komagata Maru* case. Yet he did make many decisions on his own hook and, taking his professional background into account, I think he did admirably well.

"One of his own decisions stopped the passengers from coming ashore. Another man in Reid's shoes might have choked the streets with police and militia and shot every Hindu on sight. His solution was much more sensible. On the night of July 9, he had the *Winimac* transport enough boxes of food and barrels of water to the *Komagata Maru* to last the Hindus two or three days."

The jubilant passengers ripped open the boxes and held a huge feast on the deck. What they did not discover until the next day was that Reid was not sending them free food and water as they supposed. He had urged Mayor Baxter to do so, but he was as doggedly determined as ever not to spend a penny of Immigration Department money to fill the Asians' stomachs.

On July 10 the inspector revealed that he no longer expected Gurdit Singh to pay for the groceries—he expected Captain Yamamoto to. The skipper received a bill from the grocers, W. H. Malkin and Company, and a statement informing him the Immigration Department felt it was his job to make sure everyone on the ship ate well. Reid emphasized the importance of settling the Malkin account promptly.

The captain passed the bill to Gardiner Johnson who, in turn, handed it back to Reid, insisting that the

government or the co-charterers should defray it. The
bill went unpaid.

In a July 10 communiqué to Scott in Ottawa, the
inspector resurrected the proposal that the police shanghai the passengers onto a CPR steamer. The *Empress of
India*'s sister ship, *Empress of Japan*, was outward
bound shortly, he said, and the government could buy
passages at a reduced rate. Again, Scott issued a firm
and disappointing no.

When the new rations ran out on July 11, the
inspector ordered more food and water, adding the cost
to the ship owners' unsolicited account at Malkins.
Though the Immigration Department was not paying
the shot, Reid was not a generous provider. He fed the
passengers grudgingly, his annoyance at having to feed
them at all evident in the shortness of his shopping list.
The Punjabis got just enough provisions to ensure they
did not die of starvation.

The Komagata Maru Committee wrote a series of
letters protesting their sparse rations. Reid ignored
them. He had correctly surmised that the East Indians
would be incensed about the short supplies but, their
hunger pangs sharply decreased, they would not rush
ashore in lifeboats.

One of the committee's letters also said there was not
sufficient water to raise steam and operate the lighting
system, and Reid was urged to remedy "the dirtiness of
the ship, otherwise there will be a fear of serious sickness." Another letter appealed for a daily medical
inspection by an immigration doctor. Dr. Singh obviously was not permitted to leave his cabin no matter
how badly his services were needed.

Reid snubbed the committee's requests, but he
responded immediately to a message he got July 11

from Dr. Singh. The physician's pleading missive said:

"I have already informed you many times of my position on the ship. My life is in danger, they may strike at any moment. I cannot stand their insults and am sorry to have nothing to defend me. I don't mind if I can't land. Kindly send me back to India by another steamer, I am willing to pay the fare. Have you no pity? For God's sake save me from this and get me off this ship. Kindly do something or I am lost."

Reid's rejoinder advised Dr. Singh that he would be taken off the ship in a few days to attend a Board of Inquiry hearing. The hearing, he said, would be an excuse for having a private chat. Reid enclosed a whistle for the doctor to blow in case of assault: once the guards on the immigration launch heard the whistle they would rush to his rescue. Fortunately for him, Dr. Singh had no cause to blow the whistle and, keeping his word, the inspector had the *Winimac* pick him up on July 13. The doctor and his family were released without a fuss when the immigration guards boarded the vessel. But Gurdit wrote Reid a letter giving two reasons why he thought Dr. Singh should be denied entry. The doctor was a ship's employee under contract to the co-charterers, he said, and he lied in telling an immigration officer he had one wife—he had a second bride in India.

Dr. Singh's case was accorded top-priority treatment. The day the guards took him ashore, the Board of Inquiry waved its magic wand and the much-harassed physician was transformed into a bona-fide immigrant in a land of plenty. (His perpetual anxiety about being assassinated—many local Sikhs branded him a traitor—clouded the glowing future he might have had in Canada and early in 1915 the doctor went back to Hong Kong where he re-enlisted in his old regiment.)

About the same time Reid was taking care of his ship-board informant, telegraph wires between Ottawa and Vancouver were humming with messages slugged *Rush, Confidential.* A new player in the *Komagata Maru* game, Sir Charles Hibbert Tupper, was by-passing Scott and Stevens and dealing directly with Prime Minister Borden.

A Harvard-educated lawyer, Tupper was hired by Gardiner Johnson to try and unscramble the mess that apparently had everybody else stymied. The 59-year-old Tupper had held the marine and fisheries portfolio in the MacDonald, Abbott and Thomson governments and had been Solicitor-General when his father, Sir Charles Tupper, was Prime Minister. His contacts in Ottawa's upper echelons guaranteed a lucrative trade for the Vancouver law office he opened upon quitting politics in 1904.

Tupper kicked off his cross-country dialogue with Borden by forthrightly stating that the co-charterers were obligated to purchase all provisions. But, he said, because they refused to do so, the only way the government could ensure the ship's immediate departure would be to buy the food and water itself. He estimated the cost at $4,000.

Tupper's suggestion would not have gotten to first base with Malcolm Reid, Scott or Stevens. But Borden was his own man and, reaching a conclusion that un-doubtedly galled those three gentlemen, he decided that $4,000 was an insignificant sum to expend if it consti-tuted the difference between a prolonged stalemate and a swift settlement.

The Prime Minister's decision did not win Acting Interior Minister C. J. Doherty's unbridled approval either. (Doherty was filling in for the vacationing Cabinet minister normally in charge of immigration.)

But, as Borden's reply to Tupper stated, Doherty would support it if the Vancouver attorney could convince him it would bear fruit:

"Your telegram submitted to Doherty. He considers it a bad precedent to supply provisions as this example would encourage other charters to engage in similar expeditions. However, he will be disposed to accept suggestion if absolutely assured this action will result in immediate departure. Can you give or obtain such assurance?"

Jumping at the chance to effect an expeditious solution, Tupper wired Borden proposing the provisions be placed aboard the freighter once it was safely beyond the three-mile limit.

To which the Prime Minister answered: "Acting Minister [Doherty] is instructing immigration officials at Vancouver to carry out your suggestion if practicable. If the proposal can be carried out very important that action should be prompt."

When apprised of the government's policy shift, Malcolm Reid telegraphed Scott: "*Winimac* unable carry provisions. Can you authorize fisheries cruiser report here or shall I hire tug?"

Scott's terse retort read: "Hire tug or tugs."

Finding a boat capable of hauling a mountain of food and water was easily accomplished: a mile-long section of the waterfront was a nest for a fleet of powerful steam-driven tugs. With a single phone call Reid lined up a sturdy and spacious craft, the *Sea Lion*.

The Ghadrite problem was not about to be mastered with the same ease.

Hopkinson's spies had come upon traces of the mass-escape conspiracy. They learned precious little apart from the disturbing revelation that weapons were being bought in Washington State which the revolutionaries planned to present to the passengers.

In a maneuver aimed at aborting the escape plan, Malcolm Reid persuaded local CPR executives F. W. Peters and H. W. Brodie to mail him an official letter declaring they did not want the Asians housed in the company's detention shed.

The Ghadrites were disheartened but not defeated. At 1:30 A.M. on July 13 two rented gas-boats, their lights out, sheared through the darkness toward the *Komagata Maru*. The launches came from the eastern end of the Inlet where beachcombers and fishermen lived in shacks and houseboats amidst a patchwork of sawmills and canneries.

The gas-boats were sparsely manned; the Ghadrites wanted lots of room so they could fill the launches to capacity with fleeing passengers. Yet even if the raid succeeded, the rebels could not free all of the passengers and they still planned to smuggle arms aboard the freighter at a later date.

The *Winimac* circled the freighter at intervals, constantly altering her timetable. The East Indians piloting the gas-boats prayed they would be able to sneak passengers off the freighter's port side, which faced the North Shore, before the government craft, sitting between the ship's starboard and Pier A, made her next round.

Their luck held out until they were 200 yards away. Then the *Winimac* slid out of her mooring and, chugging around the freighter's bow, spotted the launches and their unmistakably East Indian occupants. The *Winimac* halted. Slipping ammunition clips into Ross rifles, the immigration guards warned the gas-boats to turn back. Awakened by the shouting, passengers rushed to the *Komagata Maru*'s bow, flaying the soft nocturnal air with screams for the gas-boats to draw nearer; they would leap overboard, they yelled, and swim to meet the launches.

The gas-boats hung on, cutting wide circles, their skippers debating whether they should streak past the *Winimac* or retreat. After five taut minutes they relented.

Reid buttressed the patrol the following evening. The *Winimac*, the *Mary Ellen* and a rowboat crammed with rifle-bearing guards were assigned a dusk-to-dawn vigil. All three crafts carried rockets. In the event of trouble, a rocket was to be fired and a constable stationed on Pier A to watch for a signal would summon reinforcements.

The Ghadrites remained undeterred. Contemptuously defying the odds against success, they plunged ahead with their gun-gathering project. On July 17 the revolutionaries suffered a jarring setback: Bhag Singh, Balwant Singh and Hernan Singh were arrested in the Washington border town of Sumas, and a fourth Vancouverite, Mewa Singh, was placed behind bars in the provincial jail in Abbotsford, on the B.C. side of the 49th parallel.

Mewa was grabbed attempting to smuggle a .32-caliber revolver and 500 rounds of ammunition through a customs checkpoint. The others were detained under police guard in a Sumas hotel room where a raiding party found two .32 Savage automatics and a Hopkins and Allen .25.

Malcolm Reid was delighted. Bhag was the priest and *Komagata Maru* co-charterer with whom he had locked horns. Balwant, also a priest, was an extremely vocal member of the Temple Committee. It was an unexpected blessing, akin to a gift from the gods, to have both agitators removed from the scene.

Hernan was no stranger to the inspector either. Deported to Hong Kong in 1913, he had somehow slipped back into Canada and was running two prosperous businesses, a Victoria grocery store and a Vancouver mining firm. He would be returned to the Far East again.

Of the four arrested, Mewa Singh seemed the least dangerous. A polite, soft-spoken millworker, 34 years old, he expressed his willingness to cooperate with the authorities, saying he was an innocent led astray by Bhag and Balwant. But Reid was suspicious: he had a disquieting feeling that Mewa was more than a harmless pawn. Subsequent events bore out the inspector's uneasiness.

Ten

PRIME MINISTER BORDEN, a modest and unimaginative country lawyer, did not possess the inexorable toughness and towering ego that so often produces great rulers. He did not have very good health either. Nervous exhaustion and recurring carbuncles plagued him throughout the summer of 1914, yet he took an active part in all important government business.

From the outset the Prime Minister favored a moderate, nonaggressive approach in the *Komagata Maru* affair and, striving to side-step on-the-spot involvement at the Cabinet level, he decreed that Vancouver should handle the matter itself, providing it stayed within Ottawa's skimpy guidelines.

Quite possibly, Borden misjudged the gravity of the situation. Those 2,800 miles separating the West Coast and Canada's power summit have a habit of blunting the sharpest of realities even today, and the Prime Minister relied heavily upon biased telegrams and letters to shape his opinions.

Had he fully perceived that the *Komagata Maru* quarrel had all the makings of a calamity that could soil the Dominion's fine reputation, he might not have placed so much faith in Malcolm Reid and his aides. But the Prime Minister thought they had the ability to execute His Majesty's justice with the utmost efficiency.

Or rather he did feel that way until the *Komagata Maru* pressure cooker reached the boiling point July 17 and 18, then blew its lid on the 19th. Those were the three days that spawned the riot newspapermen dubbed "The Battle of Burrard Inlet"; the three days that gave birth to a batch of nasty editorials in the eastern press; the three days that jolted Borden into tightening the screws on both the *Komagata Maru* passengers and Inspector Malcolm Reid.

Friday, the 17th, was a feverish day during which Reid and Gardiner Johnson tried to give the freighter a hearty shove in the direction of Hong Kong. In the early-morning hours Reid had the *Winimac* deliver the official deportation papers, one for each passenger. The depositing of the trunkful of documents on board the vessel coincided with the arrival of the *Sea Lion* carrying water casks (400 tons of water was ferried to the *Komagata Maru* that day) and a letter telling Gurdit Singh the rest of the provisions would be supplied when the boat passed the three-mile limit.

The shipping agent boarded the freighter in the afternoon and instructed Captain Yamamoto to clear the port. What about the co-charterers? the captain inquired. Had they signed a departure order? Johnson replied brusquely that the owners wanted the ship in Hong Kong and they did not give a tinker's damn about the disreputable co-charterers, particularly since one of them was being detained in the United States on criminal charges.

The captain did not argue. But when night fell the *Komagata Maru* had not budged.

Reid dashed off a sharply worded note to Captain Yamamoto saying if the ship was not gone by 6 P.M. Saturday, drastic measures would be implemented. The Japanese consul, Hori, requested a deadline extension, only to be rebuffed by Reid:

"You now ask me for an extension of this period in order to ascertain the views of your government. Since the matter has been canvassed in every respect for days I cannot see my way clear to grant this request, as I cannot see that this has anything whatever to do with your government."

The inspector's patience had worn thin. In his judgment, the consul was a pain in the neck and he yearned to get rid of him. Indeed, both Stevens and Reid figured that Hori and Captain Yamamoto were deliberately obstructing their progress in order to stir anti-white sentiment. Stevens went so far as to suspect the duo were linked with Gurdit in a plot to harass the Canadian government. Some of the M.P.'s suspicions surfaced in a July 17 lettergram to Borden:

". . . Tonight it appears that the captain has been deceiving us throughout. He refuses now to weigh anchor . . . I am convinced from the attitude of the captain that he is in collusion with Gurdit Singh and is purposely deceiving the government and the immigration authorities. Immigration agent Mr. Reid made a strong final appeal for assistance to the Japanese counsel Hori with absolute failure.

"I construe the attitude of the counsel and the captain of the vessel as distinctly antagonistic to the government and would suggest the counsel-general in Ottawa be drawn to this phase of the case. Otherwise it will result here as soon as it is generally known in the most bitter feeling against the Japanese which would be most unfortunate in view of general friendly feeling existing at present."

Stevens' assessment of Captain Yamamoto proved wrong. On Saturday morning the round-faced skipper came ashore and, conferring with Stevens, Johnson and Malcolm Reid at the latter's office, disclosed that the passengers had staged a mutiny.

Visibly upset, Captain Yamamoto explained that the ship had not sailed Friday because Gurdit posted sword-clutching sentries in the engine room. The crewmen would be cut to ribbons, the Sikh leader said, if they dared light a fire beneath the boilers.

Gurdit's distrust of Reid motivated the passenger rebellion. Pier A and the *Sea Lion* moored beside it were stacked high with boxes and sacks of food, but the white-maned Punjabi, a virtuoso of deception himself, reckoned it was a ruse. He believed the provisions would not be delivered if the freighter passed the three-mile boundary.

The captain's admission that he had lost control of his ship made it obvious that he was not a cunning co-conspirator but was simply a fretful, muddled soul, trapped in the middle of the cross-fire between two hostile factions.

At 11 A.M. Saturday, a second meeting was held in the inspector's office. Captain Yamamoto, Johnson, Malcolm Reid, Robie Reid, Ladner and a law associate of Tupper's, William Kitto, gathered in the small room.

Johnson led off by insisting the *Komagata Maru* quit the harbor before sunset. The skipper again raised the question of the co-charterers' consent and, again, the shipping agent said their contract could be discarded as they were dishonorable fellows. (None of the lawyers present commented on that assertion, thus giving it their tacit approval.)

The immigration superintendent tackled the captain next. He was liable to a $500-per-passenger fine unless he obeyed the deportation orders, Reid said, so he had better hurry back to the ship and appeal to Gurdit to lift the anchor.

What should he do if Gurdit ignored his appeal? Captain Yamamoto queried. Run a red flag up the mast, the inspector said, and a squad of policemen will board the ship and help him regain control.

The meeting finished with Captain Yamamoto heading for the vessel. An immigration officer accompanying him later turned in a written report stating the skipper got cold feet at the last moment and requested police assistance. The officer wrote:

"I took the captain to the ship but on reaching the side he said, 'If I go aboard the ship and put up the red flag, they are too many for me. I cannot do it. You go back and ask Mr. Reid to get the police immediately— 200 if he can—but I cannot raise the red flag as I promised.' "

Reid phoned Police Chief Malcolm McLennan at his home and learned that a task force of 125 officers and constables could be assembled. But the police chief would not do anything until Captain Yamamoto sought his aid in writing. That barrier was soon overcome. A Japanese seaman smuggled this letter off the ship, addressed to McLennan and signed by Captain Yamamoto:

"Having my clearance from this port for Hong Kong and instructions from my owners' agents here to depart, I attempted this afternoon to get up steam under my boilers. My life has been threatened if I attempt to do so, and I request the assistance of the police of the City of Vancouver for the purpose of making me master of my vessel, so as to enable me to get up steam and leave this harbor. Kindly furnish the same forthwith, as this matter is of the utmost importance to me."

The letter was a trifle inaccurate (the crew had not gone near the engine room Saturday afternoon) but it did the trick. McLennan placed himself and his men at the inspector's disposal.

Reid doubted, though, that 125 was an adequate number of lawmen to restrain the Punjabis. He had his staff scour parks, soup kitchen line-ups and saloons for ex-military men: 35 "special" immigration officers, mostly young down-and-outers happy to earn some dollars, were coralled in this manner. With Stevens and Robie Reid sanctioning the application, Lieutenant-Colonel R. G. Edwards Leckie, Commanding Officer of 72nd Seaforth Highlanders, agreed to equip each "special" with a Quebec-made Ross rifle.

On paper the inspector's strategy looked first rate. In a memo to Mayor Baxter, he wrote:

"The *Sea Lion* will take us to the ship while it is still daylight, around 9 P.M. Our guard will go on board immediately behind the police. When the vessel leaves, she will soon be beyond the three-mile limit and out of police jurisdiction. Our guard will then take over and the police will be taken ashore on the *Sea Lion*. The provisions will be brought out and put on board. The guard will be withdrawn and the *Sea Lion* will watch the ship out to sea for twelve hours."

The raid did not go as smoothly as the inspector's memo indicated. The first problem appeared at nine o'clock when McLennan phoned Reid to report he had collected only 10 constables. The varied pleasures to be enjoyed in a seaport city on a balmy Saturday night had devoured the majority of his off-duty policemen and those on duty had pressing assignments elsewhere.

Reid considered postponing the operation for 24 hours but the chief told him to wait a while longer, that he would somehow round up his scattered flock. By midnight McLennan had 40 constables in tow; at 12:15 A.M. the chief was on the phone saying he had achieved the desired figure, 125, and all were en route to Pier A. Stevens and Hopkinson shared the tedious wait between the chief's calls with Reid; the trio now proceeded to Pier A where the "specials" were lounging about the heap of provisions; everything except a few boxes had been transferred from the *Sea Lion* to the dock.

As the police began arriving in bunches, the inspector stood on the wharf with Stevens and Hopkinson, his cool eyes fixed on the *Komagata Maru*. It was a strange night. Windless, not a cloud in sight, the temperature a pleasant 60 degrees, and yet it was black and gloomy, the dim moon barely exhibiting the North Shore mountains and the foreboding, rumpled water filling the Inlet.

Like Vancouver, the city of North Vancouver pierced the dark with slashes of man-made illumination. Hugging the Inlet shoreline, North Van lit its streets and buildings electrically; its modern lighting system rivaled the Capilano Canyon tourist magnet as its greatest source of civic conceit.

For all of its electrical brilliance, the North Shore community could not equal for Reid the fascination of the smaller specks of whiteness emanating from the *Komagata Maru*. Newly supplied water had created steam for the ship's lighting and, at this late hour, numerous portholes glowed brightly.

Outwardly, Reid was so composed that when he spoke of the impending raid it was as though he were a milkman describing a stopover on his normal round. Inwardly, he must have been fielding an array of distressing questions. Would the passengers be scared into submission, as he had forecast, or would they put up a fight? How would Borden and the press react, should the attack touch off a riot, leaving dead and injured in its wake?

Scott had assured him by long-distance telephone that the Immigration Department supported the police action. That support could collapse like a brick wall lacking mortar if the attack was a bloody debacle. Once more he was confronting the very real danger that he would be the scapegoat, his career in ruins.

At 1 A.M. the police, the youthful recruits, a half-dozen regular immigration officers and a handful of noncombatants clamored onto the *Sea Lion*. McLennan, Deputy Chief McCrea and four police inspectors—Wilshire, Craig, McLeod and MacIntosh—commanded the six detectives and 113 constables. Police Captain Warden and Malcolm Reid were in charge of the "specials" and the immigration employees. The police and the immigration officers carried revolvers, the "specials" rifles; all were instructed not to fire a shot unless ordered to.

The *Sea Lion*, a big, ocean-plying towboat, was renowned as being the lone West Coast tug with a piano in her saloon and for having a melodious 13-note chime-whistle that could scurry up and down the musical scale. (A certain tune performed on the whistle prompted waiters in the crew's favorite waterfront pub to cover a vacant table with beer glasses in anticipation of their thirsty coming.)

The piano was not there that night. Captain Harry Robinson had ordered it hauled ashore to make room for the raiders. If it had been aboard, someone might have played it, for, incredibly, most of the invaders seemed to think the operation was something of a lark. Men laughed and jostled each other as the tug churned away from the dock. Fifty-nine years later, former immigration officer Fred Taylor recalled the lighthearted atmosphere:

"We were in a jovial mood, as though we were all going to an amusement park. I took a couple of friends along and some other people brought their friends too. It was inconceivable to us there'd be a row. We thought the passengers would be intimidated by our guns and they'd run and hide like terrified sheep."

At the Vancouver Press Club on the seventh floor of the Leigh-Spencer Building, everyone was in gay spirits when a latecomer remarked that he had met a police squad hurrying to Pier A to take part in the boarding. In Hollywood movies of the 1930s similar declarations emptied rooms, the reporters dashing breathlessly to be at the venue of a potential front-page story. It did not happen that way at the Vancouver Press Club. Nobody had a deadline to meet, so most of the newsmen stayed where they were, a foot up on the bar rail or their minds locked into one of several poker games under progress in the smoky room.

Four who managed to tear themselves away from the club included *Province* sports editor Jimmy Hewitt. He said afterward that he and his pals gathered it might be "terrific fun" to board the ship and "gander at the 'exotic' Hindus the whole town was talking about."

The merriment faded the moment the *Sea Lion* reached the *Komagata Maru* and, idling her engine, lay parallel to the freighter's starboard, a three-foot-wide gap of water between the vessels. What stifled the fun was the sudden realization that, owing to a tactical blunder—for which Malcolm Reid was subsequently blamed—the strike force was at an alarming disadvantage: the *Sea Lion*'s deck was 15 feet lower than the freighter's!

An awesome line of Punjabis, three and four deep in some places, manned the railing; every adult male, even those on the sick list, had swarmed topside to repel the invaders.

A Sikh priest picked Hopkinson out of the mob and, in Punjabi, hurled a warning at him. The men on the *Sea Lion* would be thoroughly thrashed, he said, if they tried to board the freighter.

Hopkinson scoffed at the admonition. But after he translated it for Reid, the inspector hesitated, his gaze on the scowling Asians jamming the railing.

Standing beside Reid against the wheelhouse wall, Stevens felt an urge to have the expedition called off. The East Indians' height advantage was a colossal oversight that could, he thought, cost the raiders dearly in terms of physical harm. He decided to talk to the inspector, but before he could say his piece, McLennan launched an attack. Policemen began tossing grappling hooks up at the *Komagata Maru* railing. Most of the iron-clawed devices were off-target and the Punjabis silently flung them back down. Then one caught hold and the line went taut.

At the same time, McLennan hustled through the *Sea Lion* crowd, dragging the limp high-pressure hose used to wash the tug's deck. An East Indian was closing in on the grappling hook, bent on hacking the heavy rope to shreds with an axe, when Captain Robinson pumped water into the hose: the cold stream leaping from the tube struck the axeman, driving him backward. Holding the nozzle, McLennan played water along the railing.

The introduction of the hose and its drenching rampage precipitated an unexpectedly fierce response from the passengers. An ear-hurting shriek, born of spoiled dreams and bodily deprivation, erupted from the throats of the three hundred and fifty-odd Punjabis. Accompanying the anguished cries was a downpour of deadly objects—huge lumps of coal, bricks ripped from boiler seatings, saloon chairs, scrap metal, hardwood torn from walls, clubs carved from driftwood, and improvised spears (swords, knives and meat cleavers attached to the tips of 10-foot bamboo poles). A constable hoisting himself up the grappling line fell, a spear in his shoulder; two other policemen were also victims, one taking a blade in the groin, his companion sustaining a leg wound.

The East Indians' furious assault caused a panic. En masse, the raiders rushed to the *Sea Lion*'s leeside, almost capsizing the boat. Fred Taylor remembered the stampede and its near-consequence:

"Just about every man on the boat ran for cover. They wanted to get inside or behind the cabin or at least to put as much distance as possible between themselves and the fusillade. We were lucky we didn't all topple overboard when the tug listed. The tide was going out and it had a strong undertow. I'm sure lots of fellows would've drowned."

One invader did go over the side, Detective Dan McArthur. It was not the listing that dumped him into the Inlet, it was a brick on the head. He was retrieved by Hopkinson and an immigration "special."

The Asians had been storing up make-shift ammunition for weeks. Projectiles continued to descend but, after the initial flurry, the density of the bombardment lightened and, prodded by Reid, Captain Warden and the police inspectors, the raiders spread out over the littered deck.

McLennan had stood his ground. His face was badly gashed and his body would bear enormous bruises but he did not leave the streaming hose. Inspectors MacIntosh and McLeod remained beside him; MacIntosh suffered several head blows, nearly knocking him unconscious, and McLeod received an arm injury when a hefty chunk of coal struck him.

The high-volumed shriek that opened the skirmish gave way to a noisy chorus of a lower pitch: a Sikh priest and a group of passengers chanted an East Indian song citing the glories of battleground bravery, combatants shouted curses and threats, and someone could be heard repeatedly shouting that the police wanted to jail Gurdit Singh and deport the passengers without a scrap of food.

Five minutes flashed past. The raiders were now scooping up the Punjabis' missiles and flinging them back. Constable Duncan McKinnon saw an East Indian throw the brick that grazed his scalp. Collecting the brick, he looked for the culprit and, sighting him in the second row, bided his time until the Asian was at the railing again. A star hurler on the police baseball team,

McKinnon cranked up and released a toss that scored a thudding hit on the startled Punjabi's chest, dropping him to the deck.

Just as the steady blast of water was discouraging the soaked passengers—their offensive was growing noticeably weaker—the pumps faltered, the pressure slackened and, although still dousing the white-clad figures, the hose was no longer the harsh dissuader it had been. This loss of potency recharged the Punjabis' flagging vigor, and they added new weapons to their arsenal. A tall Sikh, his feet on the lower rung, leaned over the rail and, swinging a flatiron tied to a long metal bar, bowled down a line of policemen. Marline spikes, capstan bars, oars and other pieces of nautical gear joined the deluge.

Inside the *Sea Lion* wheelhouse, Dr. Monro and a police surgeon, Dr. Patton, patched up the wounded as best they could: they had not come prepared to practice battle-zone medicine. Splintered glass from the portside windows covered the floor and patients frequently ducked to avoid objects flying into the cabin.

Four shots rang out. Komagata Maru Committee member Hernam Singh was firing a rusty revolver, a souvenir of his British Army days, at the invaders. Amazingly, no one was hit. As equally amazing, none of the raiders, in the heat of the conflict, disobeyed the pre-attack order to refrain from shooting and returned the fire. One young "special" nearly did, however. A kneeling recruit was drawing a bead on Hernam Singh when Stevens sprinted over and stopped him.

Stevens' cool-headed act was remarkable in view of the fact that a bullet had just missed his head, burrowing into the wheelhouse wall, and his small, compact body was aching from blows landed by hunks of coal and other hard objects. Was Hernam purposely aiming at the Tory M.P.? It is logical to suppose he was, for two of his shots were definitely meant to strike down another *Komagata Maru* nemesis, Hopkinson.

Journalist B. A. McKelvie, in his book *Magic, Murder and Mystery*, wrote:

"Hopkinson was leaning out of the pilothouse window; I was next to him but outside. There was a flash and a bullet sang past us. 'My God, Hoppy, they're shooting at you. It's your damned gold-braided hat,' I shouted excitedly, and seized the cap and jammed my straw [boater] on his head, and like a fool put his cap on my own head. A moment later a bullet 'pinged' past the end of my nose. I got rid of that head-gear and quickly."

Hernam's fourth shot punched a hole in the deck in front of Detective Joe Ricca. The Sikh had no more bullets, and if anyone else on the freighter owned a gun, he did not use it.

The fight raged on. Technically, McLennan was commander-in-chief of the task force and it was up to him whether or not the boarding attempt should continue. In actuality, Reid was in charge, and the raid would go whichever way he, not the police chief, ordered. As it was, Reid and McLennan were loath to admit the East Indians were doing precisely what the priest warned they would do—deal the authorities a thorough thrashing—and both were hopeful of turning the battle tide.

The water-logged East Indians made the coal bunkers their primary source of armament; a human chain twisted from the railing to the hold and coal moved topside, hand-to-hand, in baskets. Four coal-brigade toilers went at their chore so zealously they slipped and fell down the hatchway, suffering minor injuries. (Daljit

Singh later said they were the only Asians hurt during the riot, but time and again passengers were observed reeling back from the rail clutching wounds inflicted by returning missiles.)

The *Komagata Maru*'s bulwarks presented a formidable Everest to the raiders. All the same, a gritty policeman, Constable Walter Johnson, endeavored to scale it. Climbing on a buddy's shoulders, he grabbed at the freighter railing. He was three feet short of the mark. Exasperated, he decided to hurl himself upward, making a flying stab at catching the bottom rung. Before he could take off, the axeman appeared. The grappling hook sealing the vessels together had been forgotten in the excitement but the axeman had not retired from combat. Leaning over the railing, two passengers gripping him, he took a swipe at Constable Johnson's head. The axe sliced his helmet in half. The constable dropped onto the *Sea Lion* deck, desperately feeling his scalp to discover if it was intact. By some miracle, it was.

The *Sea Lion* casualty list lengthened. Constable McCall staggered into the wheelhouse, two ribs broken, his spine injured, his brain swirling from a head blow. Police Inspector David Scott was carried inside; a brick behind the ear had rendered him unconscious. A "special" named Maddox lay moaning on the floor; a spear had penetrated his thigh a split second before an airborne oar slammed into his shoulder.

As the casualties mounted, Reid faced a fresh dilemma. To stand fast without opening fire could result in almost every invader being injured, perhaps some fatally, and the defiant passengers still would not be tamed. To open fire could produce a horrifying massacre. His lack of confidence in Scott's avowed support cast an ominous shadow over that proposition. Yet the third alternative, retreat, was a dreadful option too. The expedition would be labeled a humiliating defeat, if not a laughable fiasco. Whatever course he chose, the self-portrait he had artfully painted in letters, telegrams and press statements—that of an able negotiator and a splendid leader of men—was certain to be indelibly stained.

When the riot was 10 minutes old, the inspector joined McLennan at mid-deck and announced his decision. He was taking the route that would fetch the least criticism on shore: the *Sea Lion* was retreating.

The tug's withdrawal posed another problem. Attached to the *Sea Lion* railing by a baffling tangle of knots, the grappling line had to be severed. Every time a policeman raced to the line carrying a hatchet, the East Indians repelled him with a coal barrage. Exhilarated by the knowledge that they were winning, the passengers had enthusiastically embraced a new goal Gurdit Singh set for them: when the fallen invaders far outnumbered the standing, they would descend to the *Sea Lion* deck and throw Reid, Hopkinson and Stevens overboard.

Constable McKinnon and "Cap" Anderson cheated them out of that vengeful finishing stroke. McKinnon, the ace pitcher, rummaged through a vegetable crate and, finding a large cabbage, hurled it up on the *Komagata Maru* deck. The cabbage had its intended effect: mistaking it for a bomb, the Asians scattered for safety. "Cap" Anderson, a crusty old waterfront character whose curiosity had lured him onto the towboat, snatched a hatchet from a slow-moving constable's hand and, running to the rail, chopped the grappling line in two. Her engine roaring, the *Sea Lion* bolted for Pier A.

The passengers uncorked a mighty victory whoop that echoed in the fleeing raiders' ears. Then they carted musical instruments onto the deck and celebrated with singing and dancing. ("They thought they had defeated the whole British Army and they rejoiced accordingly," Robie Reid said in his *B.C. Historical Quarterly* article.) The Punjabis' joyous fête was in stark contrast to the scene on the wharf. In an emotional environment blending wrath and despondency, the wounded were loaded into a fleet of ambulances, summoned by a CPR employee who had witnessed the riot. In all, 30 raiders were injured. The four reporters were bruised and battered but they were sufficiently healthy to journey uptown for a few glasses of Press Club brew. The night owls lingering on the Granville Street premises whisk-broomed the four, then gathered at the bar to absorb their engrossing stories.

The tales they wove in the newsman's sanctuary occasionally strayed from the narrow confines of accuracy to inject some color. In that respect, the Press Club sojourn was a preliminary warm-up for the main event, the riot coverage in the Vancouver newspapers, which was strewn with errors, distortions and flights of fantasy.

The *Sun* praised the police department's "admirable coolness and courage" and referred to the Asians as "barbarians." The *World*, the biggest-selling paper in the province, expanded upon the barbarian theme:

"To see that howling, half-naked mob of savages, brandishing cavemen clubs, and shrieking defiance at us with their lips curled back showing their teeth in fiendish snarls, just stripped the human of thousands of years of modern glaze and threw us back to 2000 B.C. . . ."

Besides the shamefully slanted newspaper coverage, the riot inspired an anonymous songwriter to whip out a ballad that became a staple of local performers' repertoires. Bearing the title "The Battle of Bull's Run," the lyrics are part of the yet-to-be-written history of the Canadian music hall:

"You may talk about your suffragettes,
    Or the battle of the booze,
    But it can't compare with the fight we had,
    On the *Komagata Maru*.

"Ye Gods, it was an awful night,
    I never shall forget it,
    Those Hindus threw most everything,
    Including coal and brick.

"The dirty rats were vicious,
    Some had lost their clothes,
    But still I thought we had them,
    When the guy turned on the hose.

"The boys were very anxious,
    To clean the swarthy horde,
    But just when things looked rosy,
    McArthur fell overboard.

"Dan McLeod was right in front,
    He shouted, 'Boys stand pat,'
    But he hardly said his words,
    When a Hindu stole his hat.

"Up spoke one old sea salt,
    Salt pepper, bold and true,
    And said, 'If they'd give me a chance,
    I'd show them what to do.

" 'Give me a box of dynamite,
    And a goodly length of fuse,
    And, believe me, I'd surely fix,
    That bunch of mad Hindus.'

" 'Look out,' the Captain loudly cried,
    'Or we shall all go under.'
    'Well, we should worry,' a cop did yell,
    In a voice as loud as thunder.

"When Sherman said that war is Hell,
    He sure made no mistake,
    For I was amongst the bunch,
    Dodging knives and boiler plate.

"All of the guys were gasping,
 When someone gave a cheer,
 And said, 'Here comes, Stewart,
 Ye Gods, he's packing beer!'

"One guy received a rotten egg,
 It filled his heart with dread,
 For the token that he wore that night,
 Was a message from the dead.

"But now the fight is over,
 I'm glad that we're all through,
 But I never shall forget that night,
 On the *Komagata Maru*."

Eleven

TO REID AND Stevens the battle was not a rollicking escapade, worthy of song, but an ignominious disaster, calling for retribution. Prime Minster Borden concurred. The Canadian voter would expect the federal government to act expeditiously, firmly and, above all, without bungling: any government that could not enforce the nation's laws, especially against a rag-tag band of unarmed deportees, might be in serious straits come election day.

On the afternoon of Sunday, July 19, Borden conferred with two of his advisers, Arthur Meighen and E. Blake Robertson. When the discussion ended, the P.M. contacted Agriculture Minister Martin Burrell at his home near Penticton, B.C., and asked him to make the 248-mile trip to Vancouver at once. Burrell, a fruit farmer with literary leanings and a confidant of Borden's, was to take charge of the *Komagata Maru* predicament. Reid was not to be banished from the scene: he was to be relegated to a secondary position.

Burrell informed Stevens of his travel plans in a Sunday night telegram:

"By request of Prime Minister am leaving by morning boat. Reach Vancouver Tuesday morning. A wire will catch me at Vernon before two o'clock tomorrow."

Stevens, who had learned of Burrell's appointment in a telephone call from Ottawa, dispatched the following reply to Vernon the same evening:

"Your wire received. Matters are well in hand by most competent corps of immigration officials. Ottawa has given full authority and all necessary arrangements are being made to adequately control situation. While situation is exceedingly grave, officials in charge are acting in commendable manner, also are fully advised by most competent counsel."

Stevens may well have been tempted to add, "Don't bother coming," for that is how he felt. In his view, Burrell's presence would be an unnecessary nuisance and, worse, an unjust imposition. Stevens believed Malcolm Reid should not be down-graded owing to a solitary tactical oversight that, afforded the opportunity, he could rectify. Besides, how could this stranger, and a farmer to boot, possibly comprehend the peculiar workings of the East Indian psyche?

Stevens and Malcolm Reid had sounded the gong for the final round in the passenger-government dispute before Burrell became involved. The two men had phoned Scott and Doherty in Ottawa Sunday morning and acquired the services of a Royal Canadian Navy warship, the HMCS *Rainbow*. So while Burrell was journeying across the province by boat and train, the cruiser was sliding out of drydock at Esquimalt, the naval base at the southern tip of Vancouver Island, under orders to mobilize a volunteer crew and to set out for Burrard Inlet. The *Rainbow* and Burrell would both arrive in Vancouver on Tuesday, July 21.

Meanwhile Gurdit Singh's passion for money had got the better of him. Eight hours after the abortive raid, he penned a note to Malcolm Reid declaring he would have the ship depart—for a price.

The wily Sikh proposed that the Immigration Department secretly hire him as a "mediator." Once on the payroll, he would order the passengers to cease their occupation of the engine room and the freighter would leave the port. He did not specify the amount of the fee he was seeking; he said only that he wanted "a reward of commercial value."

Reid spurned the offer forthwith. Calling a press conference, Reid told reporters with an air of sanctimonious scorn that Gurdit had "treacherously" sought to sell out his shipmates. The inspector's righteous tirade came the very day he committed a deed many people would consider equally reprehensible.

Reid had sent a *Winimac* guard to the *Komagata Maru* with the word that, rain, sleet, hail or riot, His Majesty's mail must go through and the passengers could still have the launch ferry letters ashore. The inspector wanted the mail delivered so that he could read it.

On Sunday afternoon Reid opened a letter from Daljit Singh to Mit Singh, secretary of the Sikh Temple. A stenographer copied the contents before the letter was resealed and turned over to the post office. Daljit's missive was the kind of game for which Reid had baited the mail trap. In it, the secretary spoke of the passengers' determination to fight and he said Gardiner Johnson had betrayed the Temple Committee by ordering the ship to leave without obtaining the co-charterers' consent. But the comment Reid pounced upon was a broad hint that the passengers now knew of the Ghadrites' arms-smuggling plot and regretted it had not succeeded before the attack. Daljit said:

". . . As long as we have life left in us we will not allow them to send this ship back forcibly, we do not care if we die of hunger. If we had *that thing* it would have been great but whatever you say we will do. Death is hovering around this ship but the Khalsa [Sikh faith] is prepared to beat it back with a shoe every time . . ."

When Reid presented Stevens with a copy of Daljit's communiqué, the parliamentarian dashed off a message to Borden:

"Have in hand letter from Hindus . . . which shows clearly collusion between Hindus on board ship and those on shore. Boasts of damage done to police and tug. Further regrets that THE THING (meaning arms and ammunition) was not on hand as expected."

Daljit's reference to "that thing," coupled with a spy's report that the Ghadrites had a store of weapons they wished to sneak on board, impelled Reid to once more strengthen the night patrol. The rubble cleaned from her deck and wheelhouse, the *Sea Lion* joined the *Winimac*, the *Mary Ellen* and the sentry-filled rowboat on their watchdog rounds. Mounted with a powerful searchlight, the tug scoured the Inlet hunting for gun-smugglers; a squad of "specials" and policemen camped on Pier A; a *Sun* writer said the armed patrolmen on the dock had instructions to "shoot if the occasion arose."

Stevens disclosed in his telegram to Borden that Captain Yamamoto had come ashore Sunday and he "now gives evidence of more willingness to assist." That was putting it mildly. Meeting with Stevens, Reid and the Japanese consul at the inspector's office, the skipper said he would do anything the Immigration Department desired if it granted permission for him and his crew to quit the ship.

Captain Yamamoto was receiving the same nerve-jangling treatment the passengers had dealt Dr. Singh. Fists thumped on his cabin door in the middle of the night and, on deck Sunday morning, he was accused of cowardice and of licking the government's boots. A crewman had advised the captain he had heard some Punjabis talking about murdering him if the police conducted a second invasion: his death, they said, could be attributed to an object pitched up from the *Sea Lion* deck.

Reid comforted the captain. He revealed that the *Rainbow* was due in port shortly and, he said, the passengers would gladly capitulate when they saw its imposing gunnery. If not, then the Immigration Department would whisk the skipper and his crew to land before any battle ensued. Captain Yamamoto returned to his ship, his anxiety appreciably lessened.

What Reid had not told the captain was that Scott had executed an abrupt about-face and accepted the twice-rejected idea of shanghaiing the passengers aboard a CPR liner, should all else fail. In a Sunday morning wire Scott said:

"Suggest that high-pressure streams of water . . . might be useful in keeping back those resisting the police and officers desiring to reach decks of *Komagata Maru* . . . Violent action of Hindus amply justify handcuffing full number if control of ship and passengers cannot be otherwise secured and maintained . . . You are authorized to deport by *Empress* if convinced that deportation by *Komagata Maru* cannot be promptly and effectively accomplished."

It was Stevens who had first thought of bringing in the *Rainbow* and it was Stevens' phone call to Doherty that, combined with Reid's call to Scott, had nailed down the cruiser's participation.

Reid would have preferred to have the *Rainbow* in Vancouver on Monday but that was out of the question. Drydocked at Esquimalt, the warship was undergoing a re-fitting for a Bering Sea excursion. Her skeleton crew could not move the cruiser across the Strait alone. By chance, 150 blue-jackets from Halifax would be arriving at the base Monday and the *Rainbow*'s skipper, Commander Walter Hose, would recruit volunteers from that source.

Without the *Rainbow*'s menacing presence, the government officials did not have the brawn to bully the passengers. Monday, therefore, was spent in fruitless talk sessions.

Visiting the freighter at 10 A.M., Hopkinson was greeted quietly, almost serenely. Standing on the deck, the interpreter noted that the Asians had been active since the raid: big chunks of coal and scrap iron were among the expendable items carefully piled in the gaps between the mounds of rotting garbage. The Punjabis were primed for a second *Sea Lion* foray; the shipboard tranquillity was, Hopkinson surmised, akin to a prestorm lull.

As Gurdit was at prayer, Daljit conversed with the lanky Anglo-Indian. Hopkinson said the Immigration Department had authorized him to put forth a new set of conditions. The three-mile-limit stipulation would be junked and Hoosain Rahim and Mit Singh could speak to the passengers from a provision-laden scow anchored alongside the *Komagata Maru*. If Rahim consented to signing a departure order, the provisions would be transferred onto the freighter. Daljit demurred. The supplies should be placed on the freighter first, he said, and then the parlay with Rahim and Mit should be arranged.

Hopkinson countered that the department would never endorse such a proposition and, as peacefully as it began, the discussion was terminated.

The unyielding posture struck by Daljit rankled the inspector, but it did not perturb him as much as the telephone conversation he had with Scott. The immigration superintendent told Reid some of the eastern newspapers, which exerted far more influence in government circles than the Vancouver dailies, had printed editorials in their Monday editions roasting the government for botching the *Komagata Maru* raid. The *Ottawa Citizen*, for example, said:

". . . Sending a tug laden with police and armed gunmen to deal with the Hindus is surely the limit of comic-opera government . . . It is hoped that . . . someone responsible for the government of Canada has taken action to stop more buffoon campaigns against the Hindus . . . The shipload at Vancouver were not sent there . . . to become targets for hilarious hoseplayers . . ."

The editorialist apparently did not know of Burrell's appointment but he did know of the *Rainbow*'s call to duty. He knew, and he disapproved:

"To use the little British-Canadian cruiser against British Indian subjects would seem to be the height of inconsistent Imperialism."

Maybe so, but what concerned Borden was not that the cruiser was being used: he was worried about how she was being used. In a telegram to Stevens, he cautioned:

"It is our intention to enforce the law firmly and effectively but with no unnecessary violence."

Undoubtedly, the "comic-opera" charge did not settle well with the Prime Minister. Yet it probably settled a lot better than the repulsive possibility that spurred his telegram to Stevens: the last thing Borden wanted was a brusque and ruthless massacre.

Twelve

MAT SLOPER WAS surprised. Opening the front door at nine o'clock Tuesday morning, he encountered a dozen males, some stylishly garbed, others in workmen's bib overalls, and all united in a common cause: they were yearning for booze.

The unexpected appearance of the early drinkers marked the advent of a day-long siege, the likes of which Sloper's establishment, the Grandview Hotel bar, had never experienced. By noon the waterfront pub was crammed with swilling customers and late-comers had to elbow or cajole their way onto the premises. Sloper and six bartenders, shirt sleeves rolled up, sweat dripping from their bodies, labored nonstop to satisfy the thirsts of the crowd. The air stank of tobacco and beer; the big room pulsed with the sounds of sporadic singing, tinkling cash registers and boisterous conversation. Around 2 P.M. a horse-drawn wagon from the neighboring Red Cross Brewery replenished the pub's diminished suds supply.

The cause of this business bonanza was the arrival of the HMCS *Rainbow*. Her twin stacks spewing vapor, the lean, gray-plated cruiser cut into Burrard Inlet at 8:15 A.M. and sank her anchor 200 yards off the *Komagata Maru*'s port side. The Punjabi passengers cheered and waved at the blue-jackets, but their display of bravado was a subterfuge designed to hide their alarm and dismay.

Understandably, Vancouver's white populace regarded the *Rainbow* differently: they were thoroughly delighted. An estimated 30,000 persons, anticipating a naval engagement that would vanquish the despised Asians, cast aside job and household tasks and flocked to urban rooftops, fire escapes and windows affording clear views of the harbor spectacle. Situated opposite the CPR station, Sloper's bar had the good fortune to be the pub closest to Pier A and the two vessels.

Apart from office buildings and sheds in the vicinity, thousands of human ants blackened waterfront streets and wharfs and an array of small crafts dotting the Inlet. The roofs of three city landmarks, the Hotel Vancouver and Woodward's and Spencer's department stores, attracted hundreds of onlookers. The five-story Woodward's edifice had something else going for it besides height. The Hastings Street emporium was located next door to the Marlboro Cafeteria, an eatery renowned for tasty, low-cost meals and the big Home Cooking sign decorating its façade. In the afternoon many spectators, hungry but reluctant to give up their places, dispatched friends or relatives to take out Marlboro lunches on borrowed plates and in brown paper bags. Hearing of this, a Spencer's manager decided Woodward's might not mind having its audience fill the cafeteria's coffers but he did not want his harbor-watchers buying their food elsewhere. A temporary service was inaugurated with white-coated waiters delivering piping-hot meals from Spencer's main dining room to the roof of the Cordova Street store. All the while a live-wire Spencer's clerk chalked up record sales peddling field glasses on the roof.

The weather was faultless—brilliant sunshine, an azure sky and cooling breezes—and the multitudes bubbled with a holiday spirit, as though they had been allotted a second Dominion Day. The Grand International tug-o-war this time, however, held the dark promise of a fierce contest between two ships and, beyond a doubt, the Canadian color-bearer was the odds-on favorite to win.

Not that the cruiser was a magnificent vessel. Built in 1893, the 3,600-ton *Rainbow* was a clunker by prevailing military standards. The creation of the British Royal Navy's super-battleship, the *Dreadnought*, and the emergence of faster cruisers made her sadly obsolescent. In 1910 the Laurier government bought the *Rainbow* and another cruiser, the *Niobe*, from the British Admiralty as a stepping-stone toward establishing a modern Canadian navy. Both were deemed training ships; Laurier's grand design, which Borden later wrecked, specified that officers and men were to train aboard the Apollo-class vessels for the five cruisers and six destroyers Canada would eventually build. The *Rainbow* was based at Esquimalt, the *Niobe* at Halifax.

Her combat flaws notwithstanding, the *Rainbow* was more than a match for the unarmed *Komagata Maru*. Her arsenal comprised two six-inch and six four-inch guns, four 12-pounders and two 14-inch torpedo tubes. The *Rainbow*'s ammunition consisted of old-fashioned shells; she had none of the high-explosive articles the British and German navies possessed. But the effectiveness of the ship's shells was of scant concern to Commander Hose. He had ordered crewmen to strip the tarpaulins off the guns when the *Rainbow* anchored, but that was merely a scare tactic: he had resolved not to load and fire them until all other alternatives were exhausted.

Malcolm Reid, Stevens and Robie Reid agreed with the commander. The trio spearheaded a large delegation that rode the *Sea Lion* to the *Rainbow* at 8:30 A.M. Tuesday. (Hopkinson, Gwyther, Dr. Monro, Police Chief McLennan, Fire Chief Carlisle, several newspapermen and two army officers, Colonel Duff-Stuart and Major Tobin, were also present.) The immigration inspector was in charge; Burrell's train had not yet pulled into the CPR station.

The military brass represented the 200 soldiers lining Pier A and spilling over onto Burrard Street. At the crack of dawn, members of the Irish Fusiliers, the 72nd Seaforth Highlanders and the Sixth Regiment (the Duke of Connaught's Own Rifles) left their barracks and marched to the water's edge, black boots gleaming, uniforms smartly pressed, the barrels of their rifles and Maxim machine guns shining in the sunlight. Mayor Baxter had called out the militia to control the whites on shore, whom he feared might riot, and to lend a helping hand should the men on the *Rainbow* have to board the freighter and handcuff the passengers.

Under the command of Major Ogilvy, 75 soldiers from Victoria's Work Point Barracks were already aboard. So were federal attorney W. H. D. Ladner and immigration officer Paul Howard. Earlier, Ladner and Howard had gone to the capital city to arrange for a loan of provincial police handcuffs and leg irons, which were now stowed in the cruiser's hold.

Commander Hose, a clean-cut 39-year-old missionary's son who, in the best of naval tradition, was born at sea, met the shore delegation in his cabin. The parlay lasted less than an hour. Afterward, Malcolm Reid penned this report to Scott:

"Commander Hose seemed well-informed on the whole situation and advised us of his plans, viz., to run alongside the *Komagata Maru* and drop three gangplanks, on board the poop, the bridge and the forecastle. He had two fire hoses ready at each gangplank, to be used if the Hindus refuse to allow militia aboard ship. Marines and militia were to board with fixed bayonets . . . He further planned to drive them in small batches aboard the *Rainbow*, where they could be made prisoners. Prior to making an attack, the conference agreed with my suggestion to make a final effort to placate the Hindus by getting a committee of shore Hindus if possible to confer together with the official interpreters of the Immigration Department."

When the *Rainbow* conference concluded, Reid and Stevens went to the Immigration Building. The inspector telegraphed his report to Scott, then telephoned Temple secretary Mit Singh. Reid proposed that Mit, Sohan Lal and other Temple Committee spokesmen sit down with Hopkinson and hammer out some sort of settlement both the government and the passengers could accept. When informed of the proposal, Lal came to the phone and uttered a flat no. He said the shore Sikhs would never discuss anything with the "despicable" Hopkinson, and the only meeting they would attend would be with Gurdit Singh on board the freighter.

Reid, of course, was dead set against having the Temple Committee board the ship. But with Borden and the pitiless eastern press breathing down his neck, he now had to explore any avenue that could avert further trouble. Reluctantly, he told Lal the Temple Committee could board the freighter that afternoon.

Minutes after he hung up the phone, Martin Burrell strode into Reid's office, affecting the inspector and Stevens like a gust of Arctic wind. He had just alighted from the train, the minister said, and, having sent his baggage ahead to the Hotel Vancouver, had walked to the Immigration Building in order to get an up-to-date summary of events.

Burrell was a grave-looking 56-year-old whose severe physiognomy ill-suited his personality: he was warm and witty and a much-sought-after speaker on the banquet circuit. (He served as Secretary of State from 1917 to 1920 and for 14 years he contributed a weekly literary column to the *Ottawa Journal*.)

Burrell's qualities were lost on Reid and Stevens. Despite the friendly masks they tried to wear, the minister soon realized he was regarded as an unnecessary intruder. Reid was especially inept at disguising his feelings. Writing to Borden on July 25, Burrell commented:

"I think that Inspector Reid was inclined to be dissatisfied with the idea of an outside man coming in to judicate on matters which he would perhaps consider himself competent to deal with. But under the circumstances, it seemed to me imperative to have a man from the outside."

(According to historian Eric Morse, Burrell's estimation of those circumstances differed radically from Stevens' and Reid's. Addressing the annual meeting of the Canadian Historical Association in 1936, the Trinity College professor said Burrell formed the opinion that "the cause of the trouble was as much on shore as it was on board [the *Komagata Maru*]." In other words, Burrell figured the local authorities were fumbling the ball.)

Be that as it may, Burrell plunged right into the thick of the conflict. After listening to Stevens and Reid, he held separate parlays with Bird's partner, MacNeill, and Robie Reid. And he was at Pier A on Tuesday afternoon when 10 Temple Committee representatives came on the scene.

Malcolm Reid had asked Colonel Duff-Stuart to have the dockside soldiers fix their bayonets. The 10 passed through their ranks and, the inspector said in a letter to Scott, the glinting bayonets "had a good moral effect" on the East Indians, presumably showing them the government meant business.

Burrell went along with the fixed-bayonets ploy and the decision to let the 10 visit the freighter. Reid protested, though, when he noticed Rahim was among the delegates. But after they consented to a weapons search, and no arms were found, the inspector laid aside his objections, and the East Indians clamored onto the *Sea Lion*.

The Temple Committee boarded the freighter at 2:25 and huddled with Gurdit and the Komagata Maru Committee until 3:25. When they got back to Pier A, they said no headway had been made but another talk session the next day was likely to do the trick.

The unfolding scenario, taut and mesmerizing to the participants, was a disappointing exercise in tedium for the spectators. Sunset found the throngs grumbling about spending hours awaiting a battle that never materialized. "That there was not active warfare yesterday on Vancouver's harbor was actually a matter of audible regret," was how the *Sun* summed up the crowd's mood in a July 22 front-page story.

Other than the Temple Committee's visit to the ship, the only thing that stirred the crowd's interest was the late-afternoon appearance of an Australian liner, the *Niagara*. The long, sleek steamer had a difficult time skirting the hodge-podge of small crafts and making it to her berth up the Inlet. After dark the size of the audience, which had not dwindled all day, suddenly shrank to a few thousand die-hards.

With dusk the wheels of progress seemed to grind to a sharp halt. The soldiers set up camp on a blocked-off street; the immigration patrol boats chugged around the freighter; and, to the remaining onlookers on shore, the visible activity on board the *Rainbow* and the *Komagata Maru* was restricted to the movements of shadowy figures caught in the glow of night lights. But the docile harbor setting was misleading. Uptown, the wheels were still turning: both Burrell and the Ghadrites were industriously hunting for a blueprint that would ensure their side the ultimate triumph.

Burrell was in the Metropolitan Building at 837 Hastings Street West, locale of the law firm of MacNeill, Bird, MacDonald and Darling. A late-night consultation between the erudite politician and Bird and MacNeill yielded the latter's pledge to discuss a new proposal with Gurdit, Rahim and other East Indian leaders on Wednesday. Outlined in a letter addressed to MacNeill, the Burrell formula—devised during the minister's first day in Vancouver—helped achieve the breakthrough that

Malcolm Reid and his cohorts were unable to pull off in
two months. Because he was an outsider, with no local
anti-Asian sentiments swaying him, the minister succeeded where others floundered. The Burrell letter said:

"I understand from you that one of the difficulties in
the way of the *Komagata Maru* at once leaving this port
is that the assignees [of the charter] and others believe
they are entitled to a repayment of the money advanced
by them in good faith to the owners in the belief that
they would be repaid by the value of their cargoes.

"As a member of the government, I shall wire to the
Prime Minister asking that these claims should be
thoroughly looked into by an impartial Commissioner,
and will urge that full and sympathetic consideration be
given to those who deserve generous treatment.

"I must point out, however, that this is conditional
on the passengers now on the *Komagata Maru* adopting
a peaceful attitude, refraining from violence, and con-
forming to the law by giving to the captain control of
his ship immediately, and agreeing to peaceably return
to the port from whence they came. May I add that it is
necessary that a decision should be reached at once."

While Burrell was talking to Bird and MacNeill,
Rahim and 14 or 15 Ghadrite supporters were assembled in the back room at the Sikh Temple, a large,
peak-roofed wood frame structure on Second Avenue in
the suburban Kitsilano area. None of Hopkinson's spies
attended the meeting but one of them, Baboo Singh,
pumped details of what had occurred from an un-
suspecting Ghadrite later on.

The revolutionaries argued heatedly until midnight,
the debate centering on the plot to smuggle arms on
board the freighter. Some speakers insisted the
Ghadrites were flogging a dead horse: the *Rainbow*, the

militia and the picket boats had pulled the security net so tight they would be lucky to sneak a nailfile onto the ship, let alone the revolvers they had bought in Washington. Others said the dissenters were lily-hearted and, they said, it should be a simple task to outwit the whites as they did not have the common sense of children. And one hotheaded radical whose suggestion, oddly enough, was too extreme for the extremists, advocated renting a launch and taking a run at the naval blockade, tossing home-made firebombs and shooting at any boat daring to cross their path.

A rational, somewhat moderate plan was finally contrived. Two of the Ghadrites were married to young, slender and very innocent-looking ladies. Hiding guns beneath saris, the wives would accompany the Temple Committee delegation to the *Komagata Maru* Wednesday. There were no female guards on the wharf to search them, and besides, who would guess that such gentle creatures could be the bearers of lethal weapons?

Reid would—and did. Hopkinson's informant had not turned in his account of the Temple meeting yet and the tall Scot knew nothing of the latest smuggling plot. On Wednesday morning, when the 10 East Indian men and the two women appeared on Pier A, the inspector cast analytical glances over the figures of the demure ladies and determined something was wrong. Their hips and mid-sections were too bulky for their delicate faces, shoulders and arms. Reid did not have them searched. Instead, he asserted that they could not go to the ship.

With that declaration, the inspector unknowingly planted a kiss of death on the Ghadrites' arms-smuggling ventures. All that survived of the Ghadrite plot to garner sympathetic global headlines was the fragile hope that the passengers had the audacity to challenge the

Rainbow and the militia. The Sunday morning riot had not gained the world coverage the rebels wanted; however, a scrap with a former British warship was certain to be spread over the newspapers in England, India and every other country that counted.

The mortal wounding of the arms plot took place before a gawking audience that, like Reid, was unaware that a fatal blow had been struck. The audience numbered more than 30,000. After the overnight temperature dropped to 52 degrees, the thermometer rose to a mid-day high of 75 and, encouraged by the uninterrupted warm spell, Vancouverites resumed their harbor-watching vigil.

For the masses Wednesday, July 22, was virtually a repeat performance of Tuesday, July 21. Fine weather, troops on the docks, small boats cluttering the Inlet, and the ever-present potentiality of a thrilling duel pitting the trim cruiser against the decrepit freighter. Would the *Rainbow* fire her guns? Were the Punjabis really willing to fight to the last man? These and a flurry of similar questions kept the spectators riveted to the waterfront throughout the long, sun-drenched day.

For the government officials, too, Wednesday was a carbon copy of the previous day—plenty of dialogue and no visible progress. By late afternoon Malcolm Reid and others were wondering aloud if the lengthening negotiations were time-consuming, futile acts.

MacNeill had taken the Burrell letter on board the *Komagata Maru*. It was the focal point of a three-hour discussion the balding, robust lawyer had with Rahim, Gurdit and the Komagata Maru Committee. Around 5 P.M., following a confidential talk with MacNeill on the ship, Rahim met Gurdit alone in the older man's cabin for one hour. At the same time Burrell was on the

Rainbow speaking to Commander Hose, and Stevens, Malcolm Reid and Hopkinson were waiting at the Immigration Building with Robie Reid and Ladner.

At six o'clock, the breakthrough occurred. Ending his conference with Gurdit, Rahim strolled to Captain Yamamoto's cabin and casually handed him the letter the Immigration Department had been yearning to have him write. The letter stated:

"Negotiations between the Indian representatives on shore and the Committee of my ship have resulted to my satisfaction, and I am now in a position to authorize you to get up steam, preparatory to leaving this harbor, and I hereby give you instructions to do so on receipt of this letter."

When the captain relayed the glad tidings to Reid via a *Winimac* guard, the inspector said he would fulfill his part of the bargain and load the provisions beyond the three-mile limit. Coming off the *Rainbow*, Burrell told the inspector he thought the three-mile-limit stipulation should be ousted and, the minister having more clout, it was.

The following articles were then transported to the *Komagata Maru*: 800 sacks of W.W. "V" brand flour, 600 pounds of curry powder, 240 cases of Canada First canned milk, 5,400 pounds of pulse, 6,000 pounds of sugar, 6,000 pounds of cabbage, 5,000 pounds of potatoes, 20 sacks of onions, 10 sacks of carrots, 360 pounds of Cayenne pepper, 6,000 pounds of butter, 2,000 pounds of rice, 600 pounds of ginger, 10 boxes of Sunlight soap, 500 pounds of pickles, 1,000 bottles of hair oil, 200 bottles of vinegar, 1 box of matches; 500 pounds of salt, 760 pounds of Ceylon tea, 200 pounds of tobacco, 200 quarts of molasses, and unspecified amounts of toilet paper and kerosene oil.

The government provided 20 tons of kindling wood as well, and a shipment of medical supplies consisting of 500 aspirin tablets, 500 pounds of quinine capsules, 5 pounds of Castor oil, 10 pounds of white pine-tar cough syrup, 2 gallons of turpentine liniment, 1 quart of Eckshaw brandy, 6 quarts of White Horse Scotch whisky, and 1 large box of cotton bandages.

The Japanese crewmen were admitted to the engine room, and the smoke swirling up from the funnel indicated that the ship's boilers were under fire. While the freighter was raising steam, Gurdit made a pitch for additional provisions. The *Komagata Maru* would pull out at 5 A.M. Thursday, he said in a note to Malcolm Reid, if the extra food was delivered; otherwise, the ship would stay in port.

In his personal diary, Gurdit gave this explanation for the food request: ". . . 24,000 dollars worth of provisions were supplied to us. To copy the example of the avaricious and deceitful *firanghees* (aliens), we said we would not sail until a hundred goats, fowls and eggs had been supplied. We began to have faith in our own strength. We got 24,000 dollars worth of provisions by shoe-beating a few. More threatenings would surely produce goats, eggs and fowls."

Evidently, the patriarchal Sikh was striving to practice a bit of one-upmanship over the government. Skinning the authorities out of costly provisions would make the bitter pill of the passengers' defeat a little easier to swallow. That is probably why numerous items put aboard the freighter in the seven-o'clock shipment were superfluous. The 200 pounds of tobacco, for instance. The Sikhs did not smoke and, if some of the 17 Muslims on the ship did, they would have to puff themselves silly to use that much weed.

Given Gurdit's affection for the almighty dollar, it is not uncharitable to speculate that his bid to overstock the ship may have had a dual purpose. How doubly sweet his sense of one-upmanship would be if he could sell the leftovers at a handsome profit in Hong Kong!

Reid was of the opinion that Gurdit was simply attempting to delay the ship's exit again. Hopkinson's most reliable informant, Bela Singh, and Dr. Raghunath Singh both phoned the inspector to say they felt the vessel would not leave peaceably. Later Wednesday night, Malcolm Reid, Burrell, Stevens, Colonel Duff-Stuart, Robie Reid, Bird and MacNeill all gathered at the inspector's office. The inspector said he was sure Gurdit was stalling and the government would be foolish to give him more food. MacNeill then cut short what might have evolved into another prolonged provisions hassle: he announced that he had spoken to some East Indian leaders on shore and, believing the passengers needed the extra supplies, they had assented to pay for them. The *Sea Lion* took the additional provisions to the freighter around 10 o'clock that night.

The conference in Reid's office finished with all present approving of a recommendation made by Commander Hose. Speaking individually to Burrell and Malcolm Reid earlier in the day, the *Rainbow* skipper had suggested a new offensive. Should the *Komagata Maru* show no sign of leaving at 5 A.M. Thursday, the *Rainbow* would try to pick up the freighter's anchor cable and tow the ship to the three-mile boundary. Then, if the *Komagata Maru* did not head for the open sea, the sailors and the militia would board her and handcuff the passengers for deportation.

The inspector and Hopkinson spent the night on the *Sea Lion*. Boarding the tug at 1:30 A.M., they got in two

hours' sleep. Rahim, Mit Singh and other Temple Committee members had remained overnight on the *Komagata Maru*; the *Winimac* ferried them ashore at 4 A.M.
while Hopkinson and Reid, gulping coffee and yawning,
watched from the *Sea Lion*.

Forty-five minutes later, the *Sea Lion* deposited an
icy-nerved pilot, Barney Johnson, on the *Komagata
Maru* gangway. The passengers were out in full force.
Hundreds of brown faces scowled down at the immigration officers and the tugboat crew. Reid muttered a
solemn "Good luck" as Johnson left the tug. The pilot
marched up the gangway, asked where he could find
Captain Yamamoto and vanished into the midst of the
unfriendly mob.

The *Sea Lion* drew back to a safe distance. White
wood smoke trickled from the freighter's black funnel
but that did not necessarily mean the ship was
departing. Her anchor was buried in Burrard Inlet, her
engine was silent.

As the pallid light of a blossoming dawn spread across
the city, an amazing sight was revealed. In spite of two
days of humdrum, disappointing vigilance—and in spite
of the ungodly hour—thousands of Vancouverites
covered waterfront streets and rooftops. There were
fewer spectators than there had been Tuesday and Wednesday (one reporter said roughly 12,000 persons were
on hand) but Reid was astonished to see any at all. He
had plumped for the 5 A.M. deadline because he
reckoned the populace would be fast asleep and thus the
threat of a dockside riot would be dispelled. (An un-
founded rumor published in a local daily Wednesday
night had prodded many of the whites out of bed. The
rumor claimed that when the deadline expired, the
passengers were going to hurl Captain Yamamoto and

his crew overboard, then take on the soldiers standing by on shore for the third straight morning.)

At 4:45, Commander Hose walked onto the *Rainbow* deck, flanked by a knot of junior officers. Simultaneously, a squad of blue-uniformed seamen scrambled up from below and, responding to an officer's staccato order, assumed a battle-stations formation around the cruiser's forward gun, a 12-pounder. Commander Hose and his officers stood beside the hefty weapon, facing the *Komagata Maru*. To all intent and purposes, the *Rainbow* gunners had their fingers on the trigger, ready to lob shells at the disobedient freighter. The slickly executed maneuver was strictly for Gurdit's benefit: the gun was empty.

Five minutes—five intense, sweaty, heart-thumping minutes—ticked off. At five o'clock, Reid stepped into the *Sea Lion* wheelhouse and sounded a single blast on the tug's blaring siren. That was his signal telling Barney Johnson to take the freighter out. Inside the *Komagata Maru* cabin, Gurdit turned to a fidgety Captain Yamamoto and the placid Johnson and uttered a sharp command. With what must have been a torrent of relief, Captain Yamamoto discovered that the white-maned Sikh was keeping his word: the *Komagata Maru* was to steam for the Strait of Georgia and the vast ocean beyond.

The anchor lifted, the propellers whirled, and the freighter began her slow evacuation of the contentious mooring she had occupied for exactly two months to the day. It took the ship 10 minutes to swing her bow and withdraw from the harbor. As she cleared Point Grey, the last blob of mainland jutting into the Strait, suburban home-owners climbed atop their dwellings to witness the spectacle. The *Sea Lion*, the *Winimac*, the *Mary Ellen* and the *Rainbow* trailed the forlorn freighter. When the flotilla passed the Point, the *Sea Lion* and the *Rainbow* semaphored congratulations to one another. The three smaller craft then fell back, returning to port.

The passengers had a farewell message for Reid and Hopkinson too, and it was not congratulatory. In a gesture of contempt, they jammed the stern, waving their sandals and slippers at the pair. With prophetic accuracy, Hopkinson remarked to Reid that the unhappy Punjabis were likely to come to more grief when they landed in the Far East.

The *Komagata Maru*'s trip to the open Pacific was not without incident. Two Japanese sailors, seized by a frantic compulsion to stay in Canada, dived into Active Pass, a narrow channel separating two islands in the Strait. The *Rainbow* chased the madly splashing duo and plucked them from the water.

The *Komagata Maru* and her shadow skirted the bottom of Vancouver Island around 10 o'clock. At the three-mile boundary both vessels slowed down; Johnson was removed from the freighter and the Japanese crewmen, dressed in "borrowed" Canadian naval outfits, were plunked on board. Captain Yamamoto ordered full ahead and the freighter moved away from her escort. Circling near the boundary, the *Rainbow* waited until the *Komagata Maru* shrank to a shapeless smear on the horizon. Then she charged for home, a wireless operator tapping out a terse communiqué notifying Esquimalt that the freighter was gone:

"Passed out, Komagata Maru, under Rainbow convoy."

As Stevens had surmised, the sight of the *Rainbow* had broken the passengers' fighting spirit. The cruiser was no towboat affording the Punjabis a height advantage: she was a professional warwagon capable of blasting the freighter into scrap metal. The Burrell letter was the other major factor in the ship's departure. The lure of a repayment was too enticing for Rahim to resist, particularly after the Ghadrite arms scheme sputtered and collapsed.

Within hours of the freighter's quitting Vancouver, the soldiers were back at their barracks, the spectators had dispersed quietly and collected the threads of their workaday lives, and the *Sea Lion* was engaged in a far less hectic project, towing a log boom up the Inlet. A layer of normality settled over the city.

Unfortunately, it was precisely that, a layer. Beneath the surface, the seeds of more unlawful conduct were close to sprouting: the worst, in fact, was yet to occur.

Thirteen

FATIGUED BY A tough Parliamentary session and again troubled by carbuncles, Prime Minister Borden started a month's holiday at an Ontario lake resort on July 23, within a few hours of the *Komagata Maru*'s sailing. He was, he said in his memoirs, looking forward "with joyful anticipation to four restful weeks at Muskoka." His Ottawa colleagues were scattered over the land; Laurier had assured the House World War I would never happen.

After a week of golfing, swimming and reading, the stocky, white-thatched P.M. rushed back to the capital, an urgent telegram from his secretary in his briefcase. Holidaying M.P.s soon joined him. On August 6, the Borden regime rammed through an order-in-council mobilizing the first Canadian overseas contingent. "As to our duty," the Prime Minister said, "all are agreed we stand shoulder to shoulder with Britain and other British Dominions in this quarrel."

The outbreak of the Great War split British Columbia's East Indian community into two camps. The overwhelming majority were faithful to the Crown, many of them displaying their allegiance in France and Belgium. Immigration agents Bela Singh and Harnan Singh were among the loyalists. They offered to help form a special B.C. Sikh unit but the federal government, apparently ignorant of the Sikhs' military prowess, rejected the idea.

On the other side of the coin, the Ghadrites berated the loyalists and secretly rooted for the Kaiser. In what can be construed as a classic gambit in the sphere of political hypocrisy, several revolutionaries telegraphed Premier McBride their vows of fidelity to the King at the same time they were deeply immersed in rebellious scheming.

The Ghadrites' animosity for the British propelled them into an alliance with the Germans. In October, 1914, the movement's co-founder and chief sparkplug, Lala Har Dayal, left his San Francisco teaching job and settled in Berlin. (Har Dayal was a philosopher-historian whose brain power was extraordinary. While studying at Oxford, he read *Othello* one night and astonished a professor by reciting the entire text the next day. Not only could he recall every line, he could recite the play backward!) Har Dayal gained Germany's oath to arm the Ghadrites. But three ships carrying contraband guns to India were seized by the authorities: the failure of the smuggling plots added greatly to the movement's demise.

While all this was going on, Vancouver was stunned by a series of brutal murders. Three of the four Sikhs arrested on gun-smuggling charges were central figures in the bloodbath. Hernan Singh, the prosperous business-man who had been deported once before, was returned to Hong Kong again. But the cases against priests Bhag Singh and Balwant Singh were too shaky and the charges had to be dropped—in spite of a confession from Mewa Singh.

Hopkinson and Bela Singh had traveled down to Abbotsford on the American border where the mill-worker was being held. Mewa was caught red-handed with guns in his possession at a customs check-point. Hopkinson and Bela issued threats and even promised immunity from prosecution if he would implicate his companions, but they extracted an impotent statement from him.

Mewa admitted that the weapons were intended for the *Komagata Maru* but that was as far as he would go. He flatly denied that Bhag and Balwant were conspiring to kill any white officials or that there was a master plan of sabotage aimed against the Canadian government.

On July 25 Mewa Singh was transferred to the federal penitentiary at New Westminster. He appeared in court August 8 and was fined $50 for carrying a concealed weapon. With Bhag and Balwant back in Vancouver, Hopkinson and Bela embarked on a top-priority mission: they were to compile a dossier on the pair that would justify the Immigration Department's serving deportation papers.

Mewa Singh was approached often at his South Van-couver home and at the sawmill where he worked.

Hopkinson and Bela tried to pressure him into making a new confession—a statement saying the priests and Hoosain Rahim were plotting to kill Malcolm Reid—but he refused to do so.

On August 17 a protégé of Bela's, Harnan Singh, vanished. The thin, hollow-cheeked Sikh—no relation to the Harnan Singh who was deported—had deftly maneuvered his way into the confidence of the Ghadrite ringleaders and was feeding tidbits of information to the Immigration Department. It was Harnan who disclosed that Bhag, now fully converted to the extremists' position, was appointed head of the Ghadrites' B.C. operations following his return from Sumas. Harnan was assisting Bela in the compilation of a black file on Bhag when he disappeared.

At 6:30 A.M. the informer left the Kitsilano boarding-house where he lived, bound for his job in a Fraser Valley lumberyard. But he never showed up at work, nor did he phone the foreman to explain his absence. Harnan did not drink, gamble or have a girlfriend, and he was in excellent health.

On August 31, a tramcar driver, Pirt Warnes of 2291 First Avenue West, solved the mystery of Harnan's whereabouts. Leaving the B.C. Electric Company's car-barns on the old Squamish Indian reserve around 5 P.M., he took a short cut over a field clotted with bramble bushes and the odd tree. Warnes was halfway along a seldom-used trail when he noticed a bulky object lying behind a log. He walked to the log and, to his horror, peered down at Harnan Singh's corpse. Warnes ran to the carbarns and telephoned the police. Detective Dan McArthur (the policeman Hopkinson and a "special" retrieved from the water during the *Komagata Maru* riot) came from C Division station a few blocks away and examined the body. The dead man's ankles were tied together with his turban. Three items lay nearby: an old leather satchel containing clothing, an empty half-pint brandy flask and a blood-stained safety razor, its blade open.

Was Harnan murdered or had he slit his own throat? At the inquest Hopkinson told coroner Dr. T. W. Jeffs and a jury he could not endorse the suicide theory advanced by the police department. The interpreter said that in 12 years of criminal investigation in the Punjab he had never encountered a suicide by means of a knife or razor. Hanging was the most popular method of self-destruction, he said.

Hopkinson admitted that Harnan had been an Immigration Department pipeline into the Ghadrites' inner circle. He said five or six other East Indians were spying on their brethren but, for obvious reasons, he declined to name them.

Baboo Singh testified that he was a friend of Harnan's, having resided in the same house as the deceased. Under questioning, Baboo confessed that he too was an immigration "stool pigeon." According to Baboo, Harnan did not take his own life: he did not own a razor and he abhorred alcohol.

The coroner's jury rendered an open verdict.

Three days after Harnan's body was found, a mild-mannered and aged Sikh, Argan Singh, died of a bullet wound in a rooming house at 1747 Third Avenue West. Like Harnan Singh, he was a government spy. Had his undercover role resulted in his death? Once more, Dr. Jeffs and his jury were hard pressed to find the right answer.

Inspector David Scott of C Division said at the inquest that he and Detective-Sergeant John Jewett had gone to the rooming house on the afternoon of September 3 in response to a telephone call from Bela Singh. The burly, black-bearded immigration henchman met them at the gate. Bela said he lived on Second Avenue and he had hurried over when someone said there had been a shooting.

The three men went inside the two-story, wood-frame building. Argan Singh's body was on the floor in the sparsely furnished front room, a flannel blanket partially covering it. Five East Indians were on the scene.

Ram Singh, a young, powerfully built laborer, stepped forward and said he had accidentally shot the older man. Ram said Argan felt positive Harnan had been murdered and, fearing his name was on a Ghadrite execution list, he had rushed out and bought a revolver from a white acquaintance. The youthful laborer swore that Argan had handed him the gun, which he mistakenly thought was unloaded, and while he was inspecting it, the pistol discharged. Where had the shooting taken place? the police inspector inquired. In the back yard, Ram said. He was standing behind Argan and, after the bullet pierced his neck and burrowed downward into his body, the stricken Sikh ran into the house, fell on the floor and died. The four East Indians present said Ram and Argan were alone at the time of the shooting; all four stated emphatically there was no enmity between the two.

A doctor examined the body and proclaimed the five East Indians were lying. Argan could not have dashed into the building; he had died almost instantly. Ram's companions adroitly altered their testimony. The killing had occurred in the front room, they said, but, although they were all in the house, none of them witnessed the actual shot being fired. The closest the police came to unearthing an eyewitness was when Detective-Sergeant Jewett discovered a sixth person, Sucha Singh, hiding in a bed in a back yard shack. Sucha said he was in an adjoining room when he heard a shot and, looking through the open doorway, saw Ram bending over Argan's prostrate form, a gun in his hand. A well-developed sense of self-preservation, Sucha said, impelled him to seek a hiding place before any more guns could be aimed at people.

Bela Singh disputed all their stories. Ram was a devoted Ghadrite, he told Inspector Scott, and Ram and Argan had no use for each other. To him, it was a premeditated assassination. Ram was arrested and charged with murder. But the police case fell apart at the inquest. One of the East Indians, Babal Singh, now claimed that he had been standing behind Ram and Argan and had seen the pistol discharge accidentally. The coroner's jury declared Ram Singh was guilty of causing Argan Singh's earthly exit, but it could not determine whether it was an accident or a premeditated slaying. Ram was acquitted.

The death of the two informants jarred Bela Singh. He had stalked the East Indian colony like the devil's disciple: bold, dark, indestructible. Joining the Immigration Department in 1912, the ex-British Army sepoy bribed and intimidated Sikhs into procuring information that could oust illegal immigrants or build incriminating dossiers on Ghadrites. Some Sikhs said he was not above soliciting bribes from aliens eager to keep their whereabouts secret.

In January, 1913, a young carpenter stood up at a Temple meeting and urged the extermination of the "traitorous dog" Bela Singh. So strong was the Sikhs' hatred for him that four men dragged Bela out of a

Vancouver restaurant in November, 1913, and beat him unconscious on the sidewalk. Two months later he was assailed by a group of East Indians as he disembarked from a CPR ferry in Victoria; he escaped a second beating by jumping in the water.

His enemies were legion, yet he attended Temple meetings, lived in the midst of the Kitsilano Sikh enclave and taunted Ghadrites on the street, saying they would soon be deported. The beating he had received outside the restaurant the previous year had not frightened him. He simply made up his mind never to sit in a public place with his back to the door. But the fate of Harnan and Argan hurtled Bela into a maelstrom of panic.

If the Ghadrites, enraged by the outcome of the *Komagata Maru* episode, had slain the informers, he was almost certainly a marked man too. Like Sucha Singh, the fellow who hid in his bed, Bela harbored a finely honed sense of self-survival and, he decided, his continued existence would best be guaranteed if he struck first. In other words, Bela's galloping fear compelled him to adopt the old gridiron adage that the strongest defense is a head-bashing offense.

On Saturday, September 5, the immigration agent turned up at Argan Singh's funeral in a cemetery near the Sikh Temple on Second Avenue West. Outwardly he appeared calm but his usual swaggering confidence was notably absent. When the cremation ceremony was over, the mourners trooped along the block to the Temple. Bela lingered in the graveyard, talking to Baboo Singh and another Sikh. He said nothing about his inner turmoil or how he hoped to vanquish it.

Bhag Singh was conducting funeral rites at the altar 20 minutes later when Bela entered the temple. It was around 7:30 P.M. Adhering to religious custom, Bela had removed his shoes on the veranda fronting the building. Walking in stocking feet to the altar, the muscular ex-soldier made an obeisance to the Sikh holy book, the Granth Sahib, and dropped a coin in the collection box. He then strolled back toward the front door. There were 40 or 50 people on the premises; all were seated on the floor and all faced Bhag and the altar. Mewa Singh was chanting a hymn. Bela did not sit down. He moved stealthily to the left of the door, stopping in a corner.

Witnesses testified at his subsequent trial that once he was in the corner, Bela slipped two automatic pistols from the pockets or belt of his tweed suit and discharged a shot at Bhag Singh's spine. The elderly priest was kneeling, his eyes on the altar, as the bullet slammed through his back, lodging itself in a lung. Bhag pitched forward, gasping and panic-stricken. Then he bolted upright and staggered crazily toward a small cubicle behind the altar. Bela let off a second shot; the bullet bit into the old man's abdomen as he rounded the right-hand side of the altar; incredibly, he kept on moving.

Frozen in shocked silence by the initial wounding of the priest, the mourners burst into a mass gallop when Bela squeezed the trigger a second time. The space between the immigration agent and the Ghadrite was suddenly clogged with fleeing mourners, shoving and pulling at each other, desperately stampeding for the door to the left of the altar leading to the back yard.

Bela Singh, a man wracked by a terror of being hunted, was now the very personification of the cold and remorseless hunter that he dreaded. His eyes sifted the crowd for enemy faces. The narrow rear doorway opened onto a 15-foot-high porch and a narrow staircase. The mob was bottle-necked; in the crush several men were pushed over the porch railing, sustaining slight injuries; others were so anxious to get away they jumped. As Bhag's aching and bleeding body slumped down in the cubicle, Bela selected his prey and, using both guns, he methodically fired into the crowd. Badan Singh was hit twice in the lungs. Dalip Singh suffered a thigh wound. Uttum Singh fell, a bullet in his left knee.

The appalling realization that they were trapped engulfed many of the mourners. Unable to get out the back door fast enough, a dozen or so East Indians turned and ran in a group toward the front entrance. In their hysteria, they risked passing within 15 feet of the corner Bela occupied. Swinging momentarily to his right, he spotted Ghadrite conspirator Sohan Lal amongst the running men. Bela got off a quick shot. Lal yelped and flung himself through the doorway, cheating Bela out of another shot at him. Bela wounded four more men in the cluster near the rear door, then darted outside to look for Lal. The veranda, the lawn and the street were empty. A path of red stains led from the porch to the curb where friends had helped Lal escape in a car. Bela put on his shoes, tossed the guns on the grass, and walked to his home. He was arrested by Detective McArthur and Constable Morris Lemon less than an hour later.

Bela Singh's shooting binge downed nine people, some of them suffering more than one bullet wound. But the density of the crowd and its frenzied motions played havoc with Bela's aim and only two of his enemies were mortally wounded. The ex-soldier said afterward he regretted that Balwant Singh had eluded his searching gaze, and he was sorry that anti-Ghadrites Jawallah Singh and Labh Singh were accidentally hit.

At 8:45 Saturday night, Bhag Singh was in the operating room at the Vancouver General Hospital. Lawyer Israel Rubinowitz and journalist B. A. McKelvie hovered over him. The two friends had been en route to a dinner engagement when they had learned of Bela's rampage. Rubinowitz went to the hospital to take depositions and McKelvie served as his clerk. While a medical team scrubbed for surgery, Bhag lay on the table muttering that Bela Singh had tried to kill him. Rubinowitz and McKelvie left and the priest was operated upon. The surgery disclosed that the bullet in his stomach had damaged his liver; the other bullet was removed from his lung.

On Sunday afternoon Rubinowitz, Hopkinson and Inspector Scott were at Bhag's bedside in the patient-filled public ward. In a raspy, weak voice Bhag gave the threesome a detailed description of Saturday night's events. When he finished speaking, a handcuffed Bela Singh was herded into the ward, a plainclothes detective on either side of him. A couple of wounded Sikhs close to the door, Badan Singh and Uttum Singh, identified Bela as their assailant. Bela was brought to Bhag's bed and the old man raised a wavering arm to point a stiletto-like finger at him. Bela was the beast who shot him, he said, and he prayed the courts would mete out the harsh punishment he deserved. Bela was led away by the detectives and Bhag buried his head in his pillow, saying he wanted to sleep. It was the sleep of the dead for he never came out of it. An unemployed laborer, Badan Singh, also died Sunday.

The coroner's inquest heard a procession of East Indians testify that Bela had attacked the crowd without warning or provocation. It also heard Balwant Singh swear that Bhag had never ever spoken disparagingly about Bela.

Sohan Lal corroborated his testimony. Limping into the courtroom with a cane, the short, clean-shaven real estate dealer said he could not comprehend why Bela would want to harm Bhag or, for that matter, why Bhag would want to harm Bela. Lal explained that his leg injury was caused by one of Bela's cartridges. But he said he was attending the funeral merely as a friend of Argan's: he denied having any link with the Temple Committee or the *Komagata Maru* venture. Questioned by Bela's attorney, Frank MacDougal, he finally admitted he did the bookkeeping for the co-charterers.

Constable Lemon testified that Bela declined to make a statement upon his arrest. "I gave the customary caution," the policeman said, "and asked him if he had anything to say. 'Not until I have seen Mr. Reid or Mr. Hopkinson,' he answered."

Bela freely confessed to the shooting. However, he swore to the coroner's jury, he had done so in self-defense. He was depositing a coin in the collection box, he said, when someone grabbed the Holy Sword off the altar and aimed a vicious swipe at him. At the same instant, he said, a second Sikh produced a pistol and discharged a bullet that whistled past his ear. To save his skin, Bela said, he whipped out the revolvers and fired into the crowd.

The jury held Bela responsible for the death of Bhag and Badan. The prosecutor's office formally tagged him with two counts of murder and his trial was slated for October 21.

Hopkinson did not take the stand at the inquest. Speaking at a press conference later, he said the Immigration Department had fired Bela but, in the name of justice, he was obligated to testify on his behalf at the trial. He had evidence, he said, that would substantiate Bela's self-defense plea and result in his acquittal.

Most of the reporters took Hopkinson's forecast with a grain of salt. After all, the rangy Anglo-Indian had not witnessed the crime and what could he say that could shore up Bela's wobbly tale?

Fourteen

HOPKINSON HAD BEEN leading a double life. As a skilled linguist and an adviser to Malcolm Reid, he was a punctual and conscientious worker, rarely missing a day at the office except when he was away on immigration business. His private universe was believed to revolve entirely around his wife and two small children. Hopkinson had met and wed Constance Frye, a plump and pretty stenographer from London's Highgate district, in Vancouver. Emulating other married couples, the Hopkinsons dreamed of an early retirement and world travel. From a starting wage of $100 a month when he came to the Immigration Department in 1909, the one-time Lahore police chief had his salary hiked to $1,800 a year in October, 1913. It was not a spectacular income but it was well above average, and the couple were able to save a healthy nest egg, which they directed into the purchase of a $4,000 house in the Grandview area. The Hopkinsons rented out the Grandview place and in August, 1914, they moved into a two-story, wood-frame house at 2526 Fifth Avenue West in Kitsilano. When they owned both buildings outright, they planned to retire, living off the rent. Their Fifth Avenue home was a warm and comfortable spot with a wide veranda facing the tree-lined street, oak-paneled dining and sitting rooms and an oak-banistered staircase rising to two bedrooms and a study.

As an undercover spy, Hopkinson dwelt in surroundings vividly contrasting the pleasant Kitsilano house. He occupied a filthy one-room shack on the north bank of the Fraser River in South Vancouver, a suburb densely populated with Asian and European immigrants toiling in the sawmills and lumberyards that, like an incurable disease, infested both sides of the river, destroying once-lush farmland.

Sitting on a weed and rubble-strewn lot, the shack was in such a dilapidated condition that it seemed as though a heavy rainfall could flatten it. The roof and walls were made of rotting timbers, packing crates and cardboard boxes; the window was covered with a gunnysack at night and the hingeless door had to be lifted open and shut. On his evenings away from Kitsilano, Hopkinson slept on a narrow cot and cooked skimpy meals on a rusty coal and wood stove. By his sorrowful abode, it would have taken an oracle to guess that he was anyone other than the person he said he was— Narain Singh, a penniless, jobless laborer from Lahore reduced to miserable poverty and blaming his woes on the white man's government.

His impersonation required him to look the part. He darkened his already swarthy complexion with a grease and berry preparation, wore ragged pajama-like clothing, a turban and a fake beard. In this disguise he wandered about the East Indian community all summer long, befriending seditionists and voicing an anti-white litany that he trusted would bring him to the attention of the Ghadrite ringleaders. It did not. But it did enable him to pinpoint a Victoria bomb factory (the bombs were to be shipped to India) and to tip police off about a Vancouver printer garnering fat fees for clandestinely publishing treasonous literature.

Hopkinson intended to testify that "Narain Singh" had also been at a large Temple gathering in which Bhag Singh and Sohan Lal preached Ghadrite doctrine and called for the assassination of Bela, Malcolm Reid, Hopkinson and Stevens. Hopkinson was going to tell the court that Bhag had suggested Bela be slain at Argan's funeral. A few days after the temple shooting inquest, the bare bones of Hopkinson's impending testimony were exposed in the press, thanks to a leak from inside the Immigration Department.

The revelation of his masquerade amazed many people. The interpreter had let Malcolm Reid and Constance in on his secret but purposely kept it from everyone else so as to avoid a security leak. (Reid frequently picked Hopkinson up at remote locales and drove him to a house where he removed his make-up and changed into his normal attire.)

Would Hopkinson's testimony exculpate Bela Singh? The notion utterly disgusted the Ghadrites. They had lost their respected Bhag Singh and, if it could be said any worth was derived from his slaying, it was the thought that the detested Bela would soon be swaying on a gallows rope. Now Hopkinson was threatening to rob them of even that small measure of solace. Could they allow it to happen? The three-man committee sharing the leadership reins in the wake of Bhag's death decreed they could not. *Hopkinson had to be stopped from taking the witness stand.*

Mewa Singh volunteered to kill him. The stocky millworker had been groomed to assassinate one of the Ghadrites' white adversaries and the question was which one: Reid, Stevens or Hopkinson? The Temple shooting clarified the issue in Mewa's mind. Bela had desecrated a sacred building; Mewa felt he should do everything in his power to ensure that the act of defilement was revenged.

On the morning of October 21, Hopkinson had breakfast with his family and his wife's two brothers at his Fifth Avenue home. The Frye brothers were recent immigrants and they were staying with the Hopkinsons until they could land steady employment. Over toast and eggs, the interpreter suggested they tour the sawmills. Unemployment was high (hundreds of men were working as city laborers for $1 a day in groceries) but, then again, they could be lucky because countless males were leaving the lumber industry to enlist in the army.

After breakfast Hopkinson, wearing his dark blue uniform and gold-braided peaked cap, hopped a tram for a 20-minute ride through Kitsilano, over the Granville Street bridge and into the center of the city. His destination was the courthouse building, a dome-topped melange of gray stones and concrete situated on Georgia Street, adjacent to the cloud-scraping Hotel Vancouver.

A product of the Victorian age, the courthouse exuded an appropriate air of solemn dignity. A swath of green lawn, patches of devoutly tended flowers and a towering flagpole, its Union Jack flapping in the autumn wind, separated the halls of justice from pulsing Georgia Street. Four Doric columns clung to the building's façade and an exceptionally broad stairway rose to a hardwood door and, beyond the door, the elevated first floor. At the top of the stairs, on either side, perched a matching set of sculptured lions, concrete reminders of England's might and majesty.

At 10:05, Hopkinson walked through the ground-level side door on Howe Street, the entrance to the Provincial Police headquarters. He chatted briefly in the hallway with lawyer Harris Grimshaw, acknowledging that he was going to testify at the Bela Singh trial, due to begin at 10:30 in the Assize Court upstairs. Hopkinson and the lawyer parted; Hopkinson rode the elevator to the first floor and, alighting, sauntered along the marble corridor to the room reserved for witnesses.

At 10:15, Mewa Singh entered the courthouse. The millworker had climbed the 24 steps in front, accompanied by eight unarmed East Indians. Once inside the foyer, Mewa drew three feet ahead of his cohorts, striding through the rotunda, past a wall-mounted oil painting of King George V and down a corridor. A handful of lawyers and clerks, preoccupied with their own activities, moved along the passageway. Mewa could see Hopkinson up ahead, standing near a wall, his hands in his pockets.

The eight-man escort was there to lend Mewa moral support. He scarcely needed it. Inflamed by his religious and political convictions, he strode the distance from the front door to the witness room with the assured, purposeful gait of a ruthless financier about to close a lucrative deal. The East Indian knew he was the second assassin to track Hopkinson. In 1913 the interpreter traveled to San Francisco to probe the origin of seditious material gushing into Canada. The seditionists did not like being probed. One night Hopkinson was on the street when a Sikh lunged from a doorway and fired a shot at his back. The bullet went astray but Hopkinson fell to the ground, pretending to be hit, and the assailant ran off. Mewa vowed not to quit the courthouse until he was sure the immigration man had breathed his last.

Hopkinson was alone. He had checked in with the clerk on duty and was waiting just outside the witness room for B. A. McKelvie, whom he had promised to meet. He watched Mewa approach without the least concern, for the East Indian had been summoned as a prosecution witness. When he was within a foot of where Hopkinson stood, Mewa wordlessly pulled a pair of .32-caliber revolvers from the pockets of his light overcoat. Two rapid shots slammed the astonished Hopkinson in the chest, dropping him to his knees. With a spurt of desperate strength, the interpreter heaved himself forward, grappling with the assassin. Mewa clubbed the top of his head with his left-hand gun; then the other weapon sounded three times, hammering the five-chambered pistol's final bullets into the struggling man's chest. Hopkinson collapsed, dead, on the cool white floor.

The echoing barks of Mewa's gun emptied rooms up and down the corridor. Courthouse janitor Jimmy McCann reached the murder scene first. Hopkinson was stretched out, face up, and Mewa was poised over him, staring at the body, anxious to discern and eliminate any sign of life. McCann grabbed Mewa's left arm and, spinning him around, wrestled him for possession of the revolvers. City Police Detective Norman McDonald was a few feet away, running fast, when the assassin shoved McCann aside. McDonald halted. Turning his guns on the detective, Mewa inquired if he was a policeman. When he answered yes, Mewa quietly handed him the weapons.

The detective steered the millworker to the Provincial Police cells downstairs. In the meantime, Detectives Sam Crowe and George Sunstrum rounded up seven East Indians inside the building and on the lawn. They were allegedly among the eight men accompanying Mewa, all of whom headed for the exits when the shooting started. Sohan Lal was one of those arrested.

The news of Hopkinson's assassination swept Vancouver like the monster fire that took but 20 minutes to level the city in 1886. By 11 o'clock, Malcolm Reid, Stevens and Mayor Baxter heard of it; by mid-afternoon it was a topic of conversation in shops, factories, offices and homes from Point Grey to the Fraser Valley. Hopkinson had been a glittering public figure, one of the supposedly valiant White Knights rescuing B.C. workers from the Asian hordes, and his murder sparked a massive outcry for revenge.

Mayor Baxter led the vengeance chorus. He demanded a swift trial for Mewa and a beefed-up police patrol in the East Indian neighborhoods. The *Province* quoted him that day: " 'This thing must stop. It is bad enough having these Hindus kill their fellow countrymen but when they shoot our citizens, it has come to the limit of our endurance.' "

The howling public and Mayor Baxter got the fast trial they desired. The Bela Singh proceedings were postponed and the Mewa Singh trial was scheduled for October 30, seven days after the fatal shooting. Mewa's trial lasted two hours and the jury deliberated only five minutes before imposing the death penalty.

The millworker's demeanor must have had some spectators in the courtroom wondering if they had come to the right tribunal. The press had spoken of the murderer's "cynical smile" and his heartless pretrial admission, "I'm glad I did it." Expecting a brutal, glassy-eyed fanatic, they saw instead a pleasant-looking fellow whose manner was gentle and polite.

The Crown based its case against Mewa on the testimony of two men who had seen the killing while sitting in the witness room, W. A. Campbell and Paul Caldwell, and on janitor McCann's account of the East Indian's capture.

Mewa's attorney, E. M. N. Woods, said his client wished to read a statement and the judge consented. Speaking in stilted English, Mewa raised eyebrows around the hushed courtroom when he made a startling allegation that Bela Singh had solicited a $10 bribe from him at Abbotsford jail: that was all the money he had on him, Mewa said, and Bela had promised to get him a light sentence on the gun-smuggling charge.

Mewa said he had endured nothing but "sorrow, trouble and worries" since coming to Vancouver in 1908 and the latest transgression inflicted upon the East Indian enclave, the temple murders, had to be punished.

". . . Seeing the badness done there had burned into my heart. Before Bela Singh did the shooting in the temple two or three hundred of our Sikhs would go to that temple. Since then they had fallen off and they now have no respect for it and ten men do not go . . .

"All this trouble and all the shooting Mr. Reid and Mr. Hopkinson are responsible for. I shot Mr. Hopkinson out of honor and principle to my fellow countrymen and for my religion. I could not bear to see these troubles going on any longer. There is no justice issued out by the judges nor the police, not any of them, and that is why I am giving my life to show this matter up. I am a God-fearing man. I say my prayers for an hour in the morning and half an hour at night. I know my prayers have been accepted and God knows between the right and the wrong. We cannot shut our eyes and let wrong be done."

Finishing his speech, Mewa requested that Bhag Singh's children be brought into court to listen to his last declaration. The judge tried to comply but when the bailiff reported they were not in the courtroom or the corridor he ordered the East Indian to end his statement. Startling the spectators again, Mewa burst into song, chanting a brief hymn. The court interpreter, a Mrs. Dalton, explained the chanting when Mewa ceased:

"He wishes you all to know that the words he has sung are from the Sikh scriptures and say that it is the duty of a good man to give his life for a good cause and that the condition of the Hindus in Vancouver is as bad as when the Mohammedans ruled India."

Mewa turned to the judge and said with resignation, "I killed him. I did it for a good cause. Be merciful to me."

The jury filed out and in again and Mewa Singh was sentenced to hang at New Westminster penitentiary on January 11, 1915.

Six of the seven East Indians arrested following the assassination were released. The seventh, Sohan Lal, was charged as an accessory to the murder. He was in Assize Court the day after Mewa Singh and he showed no inclination to join the millworker on the rocky road to martyrdom.

"I wouldn't kill a little bird," he protested. "It is against my religion to kill a living thing."

Other than Bela Singh, the prosecution could find no one to testify against the real estate dealer and he was acquitted.

Four days later, Bela went before a judge and jury on the double murder count. Lawyer Frank MacDougal's opening thrust was a stunner: he had uncovered a witness who would replace Hopkinson and assert that the ex-soldier did the shooting in self-defense.

The witness was Pertab Singh, a four-year veteran of the 7th Punjabi Lancers and a five-year veteran of the North China Police Force. The barrel-chested, basso-voiced Pertab sat in the box and swore he had been at a Temple meeting July 18 in which the killing of Bela Singh was advocated. He swore, too, that he was in the Temple on the night of the shooting: Bhag Singh had attacked Bela with the Holy Sword, he said, and the other murder victim, Badan Singh, had fired a revolver at him.

MacDougal argued that Bhag and his associates were cunning back-stabbers while Bela was "a man of good character." The lawyer also said:

"Bela Singh was for many years a signaller in the Punjab regiment. He is a man of education and speaks perfect English. He has been here for four years and has been employed by the Immigration Department."

The Crown challenged MacDougal's "good character" testimonial. Its witnesses said Bela was an untrustworthy rogue and his shooting spree was wholly without provocation. Confused by the conflicting stories, the jury failed to agree on a verdict. A second trial was held and the new jury, dealing with the same contradictions, voted for an acquittal.

Back on the street, the ex-soldier was a swaggering cock-of-the-walk once more. The Ghadrites treated him as though he had smallpox and gave him a wide berth wherever he went. Bela mistakenly reasoned the Temple shooting had terrified them so much they would never dare lift a finger against him.

The Immigration Department had cut off his pay cheques but Bela continued to confer with Reid regularly, filling the advisory role vacated by Hopkinson. Bela allegedly maintained his contact with the department so that he could go on extracting bribes from illegal immigrants.

For all his cockiness, Bela understood there was one thing he should avoid—Mewa Singh's funeral. On a cold, drizzling January morning, the millworker was taken from his cell to the wooden scaffold erected in the prison yard. He died as he had lived, quietly. A Sikh priest stood beside him, chanting hymns, as the hangman, a short, mustachioed individual in a grubby black suit, pulled the trap-door lever. Five hundred East Indians assembled outside the prison gates, praying in the ceaseless rain. When Mewa's body was brought to them, they formed a procession and slowly walked, the coffin raised on shoulders, drums beating and cymbals clashing, to a Fraser Mills mortuary a few miles away. The dead man's wife and small son were at the rear of the procession. Bela and his friends avoided the funeral, but there were countless other Sikhs present who were at opposite ends of the political spectrum. Ghadrites and loyalists shared the mutual belief that Mewa Singh was a courageous religious martyr. (Today, the recreation hall in Vancouver's Southeast Marine Drive Sikh Temple bears Mewa Singh's name and his hanging is commemorated annually with a religious service.)

Rumblings of renewed violence were detected all winter. Dr. Raghunath Singh had tried to steer clear of the feud since the Board of Inquiry plucked him off the *Komagata Maru*. In mid-February he boarded a steamer for the Orient. The Ghadrites were planning more reprisals, he said to Reid, and he was leaving Canada because he was sure his name was on the execution list.

On the evening of March 18, 1915, Constable George Lefler hurried to an East Indian dry-goods store on Granville Street, the city's main commercial artery. Bela Singh had phoned the police station and reported a shooting. The constable met Bela in front of the store: the burly Sikh said the proprietor had been shot by a turbaned stranger now running up the dead-end alley across the road. His revolver drawn, Constable Lefler crossed the busy thoroughfare and dashed into the lane. Jagat Singh, a gun in each hand, was heading back to the entrance, evidently having discovered he had chosen a blind alley. Jagat flung his pistols on the ground when he spotted the policeman. One gun was fully loaded, the other held five empty shells. The constable took the culprit to the store. The proprietor, Rattan Singh, was leaning on a counter, clutching a bloody towel to his head. He was wounded in the face. Another Sikh lay on the floor, a bullet in his foot. Constable Lefler bundled Jagat off to jail and an ambulance transported Rattan to Vancouver General Hospital where he died.

Bela's version of the slaying contradicted Jagat's. He was talking to four or five East Indians inside the store, Bela said, when Jagat came in. Rattan whispered that he believed Jagat meant to harm him. All of the Asians sprinted to a rear door and out into the alleyway. Jagat trailed them, firing as he ran. Rattan and the other man were hit.

That was a load of rubbish, Jagat contended. Bela had promised to pay him $100 if he killed Rattan. Furthermore, Jagat said, Bela assured him the Immigration Department would fix it so that he would be acquitted in court.

Jagat and Bela related their stories at an Assize Court trial and Bela's version was accepted. Jagat was sentenced to hang on August 4. The jury recommended that East Indians be prohibited from buying liquor in Canada: Jagat had been under the influence of alcohol and, the jury foreman said, the race was obviously incapable of coping with bottled spirits. The supposition that the demon brew made him do it worked in Jagat's favor. His sentence was later reduced to a six-year manslaughter term.

Did the Machiavellian Bela Singh instigate the Rattan Singh slaying? The Ghadrites professed he did—the shop owner was among the party faithful. However, if Bela had manipulated Jagat, it may not have been his opposition to the seditionists that created such an evil inspiration. Rattan was said to have balked at paying Bela a bribe and to have warned the former immigration henchman he would crack his skull should he enter his store again. If Bela was behind the shooting, Rattan's refusal to knuckle under would probably have been the reason: his affiliation with the rebels would have been a fringe benefit.

Wherever the truth rests, Rattan's death had the Ghadrites reckoning that Bela was embarked on a systematic annihilation program, surreptitiously financed by the white man's government and endowed with the law's seal of immunity. With a regenerated sense of urgency, the revolutionaries contrived to eliminate him. On April 3, two Ghadrite assassins tailed Bela and a friend, Mutab Singh, to a cottage at 1748 Third Avenue West, directly across from the rooming house where Argan Singh was killed. The Ghadrites waited for Bela to emerge, hopefully by himself. At nine o'clock the lights went out and the pair gathered that Bela was sleeping in the house overnight. Contacting a third man, they acquired 10 sticks of dynamite tied in a bundle. At 11 o'clock, they lit the fuse, rolled the dynamite into a crawl-space beneath the living room and fled.

The explosion blew the front out of the cottage, reducing two living room walls to a smattering of plaster and splinters. Every window on the block was shattered and rocks and flying wood crashed into nearby dwellings. The force of the blast ripped a baseboard from the wall of the house next door and it struck an East Indian woman nursing her baby.

Mutab Singh, the foreman of a False Creek sawmill, was killed and Deepla Singh and Payhan Singh seriously injured. Six other men sleeping in the cottage escaped unhurt, Bela Singh among them. Police said the assassins had used enough dynamite to wipe out the cottage and all of its occupants, but the bundle was badly placed. The greatest impact of the explosion bore downward, tearing a hole in the ground and smashing a granite boulder that served as part of the foundation. Had the dynamite been thrown through the window, it was doubtful anyone would have survived.

Bela was seething mad. The cloak of invincibility he was positive he had been wearing had not been stripped away, but his enemies had drummed up sufficient nerve to try and destroy it. More attempts would surely be made unless he intensified the Ghadrites' fear of him. The day after the bombing, Bela dragged a portly, middle-aged East Indian grocer into the lane behind his

South Vancouver store and beat him savagely. Bela suspected the grocer of having supplied the dynamite. Who were the bombers? he demanded. Where did they live? The battered grocer denied any knowledge of the crime except for what he had read in the newspapers. A patrolling policeman stumbled upon the pair and Bela was arrested and charged with assault. In court, the prosecutor reviewed the ex-soldier's past scrapes with justice and opined that his imprisonment would be a great stride toward ending the feud ripping the Sikh community. The judge levied a 12-month sentence.

H. C. Clogstoun thought that penalty was far too lenient. He was the man the federal government tapped in September, 1914, to investigate the East Indian community's reimbursement claims arising out of the *Komagata Maru* charter. Supposedly an impartial commissioner, Clogstoun had worked for the civil service in India and was now living in retirement on Vancouver Island. In his report, submitted to Ottawa in November, 1915, he said that Bela was "a reckless, fighting Sikh who should have been hanged." He called the Temple Committee "ruffians" and "seditionists" and, he said, the local Sikhs did not warrant one penny of government reimbursement. (Clogstoun also felt a lack of the white man's domination bred West Coast rebellion. "Under reasonable control the native of India is amenable and capable of much good. In its absence he is as troublesome as an undisciplined child, with the capacity for mischief of a man.")

When he was released from prison in 1916, Bela Singh saw it would be impossible to stitch together the threads of his old life style. The Immigration Department wanted nothing to do with him, his comrades in the Sikh colony were fighting overseas, and the Ghadrite movement, subdued by the failed uprising in India, was no longer considered a problem by the Canadian government.

Yet the Ghadrites were still smarting from the wounds Bela had inflicted, and his execution remained a hot item on their agenda. Tipped off that the rebels wanted his scalp and, now devoid of his false feeling of infallibility, Bela crossed the border and returned to India on a Seattle tramp freighter. For 18 years, the Ghadrites financed efforts to locate Bela amongst India's teeming millions.

It seemed to be a hopelessly inane project, a waste of energy and money. But in May, 1934, the news wires carried a report that his enemies had finally tracked him down. Bela Singh was murdered in a ravine near a mud-hut Punjab village. The assassins had hacked off his limbs, one at a time, before delivering the *coup de grâce*: severing his head.

Fifteen

SHALLOW, WIDE AND muddy, the Hooghly River extends from the Bay of Bengal off India's east coast to the throbbing metropolis of Calcutta, 80 miles inland. The Hooghly has a split personality. In the winter it runs smooth and slow; in the summer it swells and writhes under the tortorous monsoon rains that slide earth into its bed quicker than dredges can scoop it out. Strong tides, bores and perpetually changing bed levels have bedeviled seagoing vessels during the summer monsoons since British traders began exploiting Calcutta's jute mills over 200 years ago.

When the *Komagata Maru* turned its bow into the Hooghly estuary on September 26, 1914, the river was recuperating from an unusually prolonged and severe monsoon bombardment. The rains were gone but the tides stayed dangerously fierce and the ship's pilot grumbled about mud banks that could snare the freighter like beartraps.

In Vancouver the *Komagata Maru* episode had not yet wound to a close. Hopkinson was still alive and playing his tricky game of duplicity, and Bela Singh was sitting in jail, awaiting trial following the temple shooting. But Gurdit Singh had other worries to occupy his mind—and the perilous Hooghly was but one of them.

Discovering he had transferred his bank funds from Japan to Calcutta, some of the Punjabis swore they would do him in unless he returned their "safekeeping" money when the ship docked. Their belligerence rivaled that of the vessel's owners: Gurdit's behavior had besmirched the company's reputation, they said, and a lawsuit was in the offing. Even more foreboding was his imminent meeting with the British lion. Gurdit had a nagging suspicion the Calcutta police would leap upon him because he had not only tweaked the lion's tail in Canada but he had done it again in Japan.

After a three-week voyage from Vancouver, the freighter had put in at Yokohama, the first of three projected stopovers, on August 16. No sooner had she tied up at the wharf than a Japanese immigration officer came briskly up the gangway and gave Gurdit a letter signed by the Colonial Secretary of Hong Kong. Concerned that the brooding passengers might incite East Indian regiments stationed in the British colony to mutiny, the Colonial Secretary warned Gurdit that they would be jailed as vagrants if they disembarked there. Gurdit took the letter to the British Consulate. With Hong Kong barring its doors to the passengers, it became necessary for the *Komagata Maru* to go on to India. Therefore, the Sikh leader said, the British government was obligated to bolster her inadequate food supply.

The consul's reply was cold and adamant. The *Komagata Maru* had enough provisions to get to India, he said, and the Punjabis were trying to delude him. A few hours after the consul's rebuff, the ship's owners wired Captain Yamamoto instructions to take the freighter on to Kobe. The ship left Yokohama on August 18 and arrived at the southern Japanese port on the 21st.

Fifteen passengers landed at Kobe and two got on— 23-year-old university graduate and anti-British agitator Jawahar Mal and his 17-year-old brother, Narain Das. Jawahar said he would be on the ship until her last stopover, Singapore. He distributed copies of the *Ghadr* and addressed the passengers in small groups, speaking glowingly of their actions in Canada. Interpreting Gurdit's bid for more provisions as a spirited blow against the Empire, he helped him organize demonstration units. The demonstrators paraded through Kobe in large numbers and, ringing the British Consulate, threatened to set it ablaze. While the protesters made a fuss outside, Gurdit and Jawahar spearheaded delegations that barged into the consul's office to badger the diplomat point-blank. Intimidated in this fashion for six days, the consul finally capitulated and wired India requesting 9,000 yen to purchase food. (An inquiry investigating the *Komagata Maru*'s homeward journey criticized the consul for sanctioning the "exorbitant" payment and for failing to personally probe the extent of the ship's supplies. "There were on the ship at this time very considerable stores of provisions and a very small amount of additional supplies were really necesary," the inquiry stated.)

Gurdit Singh spent 435 yen on supplies and pocketed the rest, telling the passengers he would divide the spoils with them in Calcutta. On September 3 the *Komagata Maru* pulled out of Kobe on a 13-day trip to Singapore. As a precautionary measure, port officials in the Straits Settlement capital assigned the *Komagata Maru* a mooring five miles from land. None of the passengers were allowed to disembark, not even men with families in Singapore.

For over six months the Punjabis had been domiciled on the freighter. For almost five of those months they had been haunted by their private ghosts, exasperation, resentment, depression. Canada did not want them. Neither did Hong Kong or Singapore. Gurdit Singh's uneasiness about the sort of reception awaiting the ship in Calcutta was now shared by most of the passengers. Would the Indian government let them disperse and meld into the city's one million population or would they be seized like poisonous serpents that must be exterminated? Some of the Sikhs girded themselves for the worst. Friends and relatives in Kobe and Yokohama had collected funds to help them resettle in India; the wary passengers used the money to bribe the Japanese crewmen and revolvers were smuggled on board.

Gurdit Singh claimed in his book, *The Voyage of the Komagata Maru*, that he learned of the arms cache after the freighter left Singapore September 19. He said that he and Jawahar gathered the weapons, throwing some overboard and restoring the remainder to the crew. With a nauseous dash of self-righteousness, he wrote:

"We were very particular from the very beginning that nothing illegal or unconstitutional should be done on our part, otherwise we would lose the moral support and sympathy of the public. So a thorough search was made . . . Before we reached Calcutta we got thoroughly satisfied that none of the passengers had anything in their possession for which we could be blamed afterwards. I also served a written notice upon the Captain of the ship instructing him to warn his men not to sell firearms to the passengers, and holding him responsible for any such unlawful action on the part of his crew."

Despite Gurdit's assertions to the contrary, the passengers were definitely armed and, in all probability, with his blessing. The leader himself may even have distributed the weapons on the day the *Komagata Maru* anchored. Whatever the case, it is certain that the passengers came ashore concealing at least 20 revolvers.

The ship was stopped at Kalpi, a hamlet on the Hooghly River, on September 27. Members of the Criminal Intelligence Department, Calcutta customs officers and police officials all searched the vessel for weapons. The guns were well hidden; the searchers found nothing.

The *Komagata Maru* was detained at Kalpi two days. On the morning of September 29 a policeman told the Punjabis not to bother cooking breakfast because a hot meal would be served in Calcutta. The lawmen departed and the ship continued upriver.

Without telling Gurdit Singh, the police had ordered Captain Yamamoto and the pilot to have the ship end her journey at Budge Budge, a shipping and railway depot 17 miles from Calcutta. The hot-meal promise was a ruse to lessen the passengers' mistrust. Alarmed and confused, the Punjabis ran to the railing as the freighter slowed her speed, veered in toward the bank and halted alongside a jetty. It was 11 A.M. and the sun shone brightly. On the pier, in a thin line, stood 27 khaki-uniformed East Indian policemen; they had been summoned from Lahore to herd the passengers to the Punjab on a special train. The arid plains of the northern province were the last place on earth the passengers wanted to go. Humiliated by the failure of their mission and, in many instances, in debt to village money-lenders, they had their hearts set on Calcutta and a new existence far from questioning tongues.

Calcutta Police Commissioner Sir Frederick Halliday and a group of lawmen boarded the vessel. Gurdit conferred with them in his cabin. Halliday swore the government was not planning to do anything nasty to the passengers once they were on the train. The sole intent of the trip, he said, was to convoy them to the Sikh homeland, thus relieving his overcrowded city of another human burden. Gurdit listed the reasons why he had to go to Calcutta. He had to mend his fences with the ship's owners through a lawyer's office; he had to dispose of the coal cargo; he had to administer banking transactions. As for the passengers, most of them wanted to earn money in the metropolis and by sending them on to the Punjab the government would be condemning them to disgrace and poverty.

Halliday was unmoved by his pleas. Gurdit was given 15 minutes to evacuate the ship. When the police officials returned to the pier, the 17 Muslims aboard the *Komagata Maru* trailed after them. They would gladly go to the Punjab, they said; indeed, they would go anywhere to get away from the Sikhs who had ridiculed their religious tenets throughout the lamentable voyage. Fifteen minutes passed and the Punjabis did not budge.

Then the ship's whistle blew and dock workers started untying her lines. A policeman shouted that the *Komagata Maru* was heading back to sea. That did it. The passengers scrambled to get ashore, carting their luggage or tossing it over the side onto the jetty. When the Punjabis were all on the pier, the gangway was hoisted and the *Komagata Maru* was secured to her original mooring.

The trickery employed to empty the vessel enhanced the passengers' anxieties over the special train. A wild rumor flitted from person to person—they would all be taken to a prison camp in the Assam region! The District Magistrate, T. E. Donald, addressed the passengers, declaring they were being held under ordinance empowering the government to restrict the movement of people entering India. Loudly jeered and stopped from finishing his speech, Donald scurried to the customs shed and telephoned Sir William Duke, a member of the Bengal Executive Council in Calcutta. Donald said the Punjabis were unmanageable and he asked for military assistance. Duke did not think the situation was serious but, he said, if they were not on the train by nightfall he would muster the troops. When Donald rejoined the gathering on the jetty and the road running beside it, Gurdit was arguing with Halliday. He was seeking permission to call a lawyer and to deposit the Sikh holy book, the Granth Sahib, in a village temple. Halliday rejected both requests.

The Punjabi constables started prodding the passengers in the direction of the railway station. The Sikhs did not resist; they ambled along the road to the depot, which was situated a block or so from the pier. Forty-two passengers went to the station and boarded the train. But the majority suddenly sat themselves down on the tracks at a level crossing 40 yards from the depot.

The police implored them to rise but they did not have the manpower to do more than mouth stern words. A priest read aloud from the Sikh scriptures, then the passengers recited a hymn entitled "Look Down, O Heavenly Father, O, Look Down on Our Plight."

The impasse deepened. The police circled the crowd, issuing commands and appeals; the passengers prayed, sang, talked and generally behaved as though the constables did not exist. Around 3 P.M. Gurdit climbed to his feet and exhorted his band to form a column behind him. Halliday figured their hunger had gotten to them and they were proceeding to the train. He was wrong. Two roads lay on the other side of the tracks. The narrow road went to the train station, the broad road joined the highway to Calcutta. With Gurdit and two others holding the Granth Sahib fronting the procession, the passengers chose the Calcutta road.

Donald sprang to the phone and contacted Duke. The Executive Council member said he would dispatch 150 Royal Fusiliers in army vehicles from Fort William barracks. Halliday also sought reinforcements. At his bidding, 30 European policemen equipped with *lathis* (long, heavy iron-bound sticks) were rounded up and sent to the highway in cars. The police squad was under the command of Superintendent George Eastwood, an overly cautious chap who concealed four revolvers on his person.

Three miles down the road, a dusty, potholed thoroughfare rimmed by poverty-infested settlements, the marchers met Eastwood's squad. The policemen jumped out of their cars and ordered the passengers to turn back. Although four or five of the Europeans wielded revolvers, the Punjabis decided that they, like the Lahore constables bringing up the rear, lacked the numerical strength to curb them. They brushed past the Eastwood squad as if it were invisible.

One mile farther along the road the Royal Fusiliers materialized. The officer in charge, Captain Moore, had his men construct a flesh-and-blood barricade across the road. The first row of soldiers knelt, their rifles pointing at the advancing marchers. Gurdit and his followers halted. Sir William Duke alighted from a car and, coming forward, asked Gurdit why he was going to Calcutta. To leave the Granth Sahib in a temple and to have the Governor of Bengal hear the passengers' requests to reside in the city, the Sikh retorted. Duke thereupon said he was the Governor's emissary and he would give the marchers' grievances a fair hearing if they would return to Budge Budge. Gurdit swung around and told his band to retrace their steps. Duke's pledge was a persuasive argument compared to the alternative, a maniacal fling at the solid military barrier.

The weary passengers practically crawled back to Budge Budge. Punctuated by frequent rest stops, the walk took almost three hours. With the soldiers following at a distance, the European policemen felt properly protected and, though outnumbered, they bullied the voyagers wickedly. Stragglers were whacked with *lathis*; passengers looking for food or water in roadside houses and shops were kicked, punched and dragged to rejoin the other marchers.

Gurdit kept the passengers company but not on foot. A curious youth on a bicycle, hair closely cropped and his face clean-shaven in Bengali fashion, stopped to inquire about the procession. Gurdit answered his questions, then bought his bike, giving him twice the amount he had paid for it. With his son on the handlebars, Gurdit pedaled back.

When the Punjabis trudged into Budge Budge the
train was gone. Sir Frederick Halliday was in the depot,
trying to obtain a second train, as the marchers swung
onto the station road. Gurdit abandoned the bike and
the voyagers seated themselves on the road between the
level crossing and the brick railway building. It was
nearly seven o'clock, the sky was darkening, a full moon
was ascending.

The police and government officials assembled on the
platform. Halliday could not locate another train right
away. Someone broached the idea of confining the
passengers on the *Komagata Maru* overnight. But what if
they resisted quitting the ship and boarding the train the
next day? Averting a riot and a possible massacre was
the officials' paramount objective—that and the goal no
one had so much as whispered about within listening
range of the passengers: the arrest of Gurdit and other
Komagata Maru ringleaders. The Indian government was
planning to release most of the passengers in the Punjab,
but Gurdit and his aides, considered public safety risks,
were to be detained in custody for indefinite periods.

Gurdit and the two Sikhs clutching the Granth Sahib
sat in the midst of the hymn-chanting passengers; the
Calcutta-Lahore police squads and about 45 soldiers
patrolled their perimeter; the bulk of the Royal Fusiliers
were a quarter of a mile away, at ease near their parked
vehicles. The District Magistrate, Donald, appeared at
the edge of the crowd. Interrupting the religious service,
he announced that the officials wished to speak privately with Gurdit. Suspecting they wanted to arrest him,
Gurdit replied that the officials should come to where
he was seated. Superintendent Eastwood, overhearing
the exchange, stepped out of the police ranks and
walked to the core of the gathering. As he stopped

beside Gurdit, the passengers rose en masse. A noose-like circle tightened around the police officer. He could be heard urging Gurdit to go to the platform, but the police onlookers could not tell if he grabbed the Sikh leader or made any other aggressive gestures.

A shot was fired.

Eastwood gasped, crumbled and fell, fatally wounded. The pistol blast ignited the Punjabis. Surging in all directions, they assailed the police. Caught off guard, the policemen slashed wildly with *lathis*, bamboo poles and swords. More shots sounded. Police and passengers dropped, some maimed, some dead. The soldiers patrolling the *Komagata Maru* horde did not stand and fight. Obeying Captain Moore's command, they sprinted to the level crossing and, framing a compact unit, adopted firing stances. But they could not shoot: partners in a swirling dance of death, the police and the passengers were a bewildering tangle of bodies to the riflemen.

With their six-to-one advantage, the Punjabis easily conquered the police, snatching *lathis*, poles, swords and revolvers from their hands and using them against their owners. The police retreated, running into roadside stores and sheds and behind the phalanx of Royal Fusiliers. Halliday was at the crossing, a bullet in his foot. As the last of the policemen fled, the passengers shooting at them, Captain Moore asked the Police Commissioner if he should order his men to open fire. Halliday replied in the affirmative. A barrage of bullets punched a yawning hole in the passengers' outer wall.

The Sikhs scattered, deserting the road for the streets and alleys past the station. The exceptions were three groups of Punjabis who, taking refuge in shops between the station and the level crossing, continued shooting. The troops advanced, firing at will, and, flushing the passengers out of the shops, forced them to surrender. Far into the night, soldiers and policemen raked the streets and buildings of Budge Budge, collaring escaped Punjabis. Twenty-six men died in the violence and 35 were injured. Twenty of those killed were passengers, including a Sikh who drowned bucking the Hooghly's terrible current. Eastwood, East Bengal Railway Company District Supervisor William Lomax, Lahore constables Mal Singh and Sawan Singh and two Budge Budge residents watching the riot were slain.

All but 28 *Komagata Maru* voyagers were captured in Budge Budge and in subsequent police manhunts. One hundred and seventy-seven of the passengers were jailed briefly and freed; others were interned for longer periods. Gurdit Singh was one of the 28 fugitives who consistently slipped through police dragnets. For seven years he wandered the central and northern regions, working under assumed names as a canal contractor, a medicine salesman and a clerk. The government never ceased looking for him and, seduced by the 2,000-rupee reward on his head, informers twice made vain attempts to trip him up. Separated from his son and tired of his near-constant roaming, Gurdit surrendered to the authorities in 1921. He was sentenced to five years' imprisonment at Lahore's Mianwali district jail.

In January, 1915, a five-man commission probing the roots of the Budge Budge riot had placed the blame on Gurdit and the passengers. The commission said the police had not used unnecessary violence, although some officers had been "somewhat rough" when escorting the Punjabis back down the Calcutta road.

Nationalist leaders termed the commissioners' report a "whitewash" and said the inquiry had set out to exonerate the authorities. The riot was, in fact, a red flag to radical elements within the various independence parties. The government was said to have savagely slaughtered the Punjabis and one tale making the rounds related that the soldiers shot countless Sikhs upon capture and dumped their bodies in the Hooghly. Not unnaturally, the English-language newspapers in India sided with the government, and the Sikh press in the Punjab said the authorities triggered the outbreak. Speakers addressing mass meetings in Amritsar and other cities said the riot was another manifestation of British oppression.

The Ghadrites mined more propaganda gold from the riot than any of the nationalist organizations. In 1915 an estimated 3,125 Punjabis streamed to the region of their birth from all over the world: "Remember Budge Budge" was the rallying cry that pulled many rebels home.

The San Francisco periodical, *Ghadr*, helped keep the Budge Budge memory aglow with a 1916 article glorifying the *Komagata Maru* enterprise. Heavy on revolutionary rhetoric and light on factual content, the article embodied this poetic comment:

". . . Foreigners have robbed our country but we have awakened from a deep sleep. Our garden wilted without water but we have irrigated it with our blood. Thou hast nourished us with the sweet milk, O mother, and now we give our blood for thee . . ."

The British relentlessly and harshly extinguished every revolutionary blaze the Ghadrites lit. Sohan Patrak, Harman Singh and Narayan Singh, three Ghadrites sent to Burma from California, were hanged for espousing sedition to East Indian regiments in Rangoon, and 25 East Indians went to the gallows in Lahore. Incited by Ghadrites Jagat Singh and Kasim Mansoor,

700 Muslim soldiers of the 5th Light Infantry mutinied in Singapore in February, 1915. Forty-eight people died during the regiment's two-day rampage. Twenty-seven mutineers were sentenced to death; they were taken to a public square, tied to posts and executed by five-man firing squads.

Gurdit Singh was applauded by the Ghadrites as a nationalist zealot. It was a role he relished. In his book he depicted himself as a gutsy liberator grappling a despotic British lion for the sake of his fellow countrymen. (Published at his own expense in the 1920s, the book contains so many self-justifying distortions that it is hard to accept any of it as gospel truth.)

Yet Gurdit did admit that he eluded his pursuers for seven years in India because he feared they wanted to kill him. The firing squad or the scaffold and heroic martyrdom held no allure for Gurdit Singh. When he faded out of the historical spotlight in 1928 he was living in Calcutta: irrepressible as ever, his old charm flowing once again, he was raising funds to launch a steamship service that would carry East Indian farmers to the most unlikely of places, the jungles of Brazil.

Gurdit's final fate is a mystery but the fate of his leading foe, Malcolm Reid, is not. The *Komagata Maru* affair did not harm his career after all. He was appointed special immigration agent for western Canada in the late 1920s; he died in 1936. As for the *Komagata Maru*, the freighter was broken up for scrap in Japan in 1924.

Unfortunately, racial attitudes cannot be scrapped as easily as can ships. Canada's treatment of the *Komagata Maru* passengers—who, apart from the roguish Gurdit Singh, wanted only a chance to prove their worth in a new land—should have shamed us into trying to understand and accept Asian immigrants. It did not. We have held onto our prejudice as though it were a cherished heirloom that should be passed from generation to generation, and the same pro-white ideals Canadians embraced in 1914 have once again set the stage for an ugly racial confrontation.

Aftermath

EVERY WEEKDAY MORNING a convoy of Number 6 buses moves along Fraser Street, past small shops, loan companies and second-rate department stores, en route to downtown Vancouver, six miles away. The passengers carrying lunch pails far outnumber those clutching attaché cases: spreading north from the Fraser River's polluted waters, South Vancouver is a predominantly working-class district and its bus-riding residents are bound for jobs in warehouses, on the docks and at construction sites.

If it were not for their jobs, many would never go downtown at all. The people of South Vancouver like to stay around the neighborhood, catching the Irish Rovers on television, taking a chance at the weekly Legion Bingo or blending into the noisy confusion of the *Blue Boy* beer parlor. New cars, fancy houses, good marks at school and Bobby Hull are admired; welfare, common-law marriage, company foremen and Alice Cooper are scorned.

Until 1971 South Vancouver was a calm, almost drowsy place, seldom in the news and preferring it that way. Juvenile car theft, breaking and entering and family squabbles were the most common police complaints. Then the East Indians poured in. There had always been some, an ignored, disliked minority. But an unexpected surge increased Vancouver's East Indian population from 11,000 to 22,000 and South Vancouver, forced to absorb thousands of the newcomers, reacted viciously.

Obscenities were painted on the walls of the Sikh Temple. Rocks smashed through windows in private homes. Youth gangs hunted and assaulted East Indian men and women in the streets. The popular slang for the turban-wearing Sikhs became "ragheads" and "Punjabs."

The incidents of physical violence and property damage are front-page news, but Canadians have been hurting the Sikhs in quieter, more subtle ways since the *Komagata Maru* departed 60 years ago. Such as perpetuating the unjust impression that all Sikhs were disloyal to the Empire during World War I. As late as 1943, our newspapers carried stories suggesting Germany had financed the *Komagata Maru* expedition in a plot to embarrass the Canadian government.

The unproven German connection with the voyage—plus Ghadrite terrorism in Asia and the Vancouver murders and riot—unfairly stigmatized British Columbia's East Indian community for years after the Great War ended.

Sikh soldiers established a sterling record on European, Turkish and African battlefronts. One hundred thousand Sikhs donned army uniforms and 14 Military Crosses went to Punjabis. Yet these examples of gallantry and loyalty were somehow obscured: white Canadians tended to focus on the outrages committed by a minority.

The disloyalty stigma and continuing high unemployment, particularly during the Depression, prompted the federal government to retain its anti-Asian immigration policy. In the 25 years from 1920 to 1945, 675 East Indians entered Canada.

The East Indians were not the only nonwhites being discriminated against. Ottawa still limited Japanese and Chinese immigration but, despite the restrictions, both groups had roughly 20,000 people residing in B.C. during the 1930s. The Japanese and Chinese were tarred with the same brush used on the Sikhs: whites said they were devious, had vile living habits and were biologically equipped to reproduce faster than Occidentals. Some Vancouver movie houses in the '30s forced Orientals to sit in segregated sections, and a public swimming pool, the Crystal, refused to admit them.

The sneak attack on Pearl Harbor in 1941 had a calamitous effect on both the U.S. fleet and the status of British Columbia's Japanese Canadians. Labor unions, M.P.s, veterans' clubs, civic officials and community organizations publicly asserted that all Japanese, foreign and Canadian-born, were enemy aliens and should be placed in internment camps, away from coastal defense installations.

Ottawa nodded in agreement. In February, 1942, the Mackenzie King government invoked the *War Measures Act*, ordering all Japanese men, women and children to be rounded up and transported inland. Private property was impounded, Japanese-language schools and newspapers shuttered, and a mass evacuation carried out. Thousands of males were taken from their families and sent to work in Ontario factories. Others labored on B.C. Interior road gangs and in the sugar-beet fields of Manitoba and Alberta. The women and children not assigned work duties were kept in decaying B.C. ghost towns or in special camps.

Countless times the impounded property was looted or sold at a fraction of its actual value. When they were released at war's end, 3,900 Japanese migrated to a devastated Japan rather than remain in Canada. The 19,000 staying behind had a lingering indignity to suffer: until 1949 they could not travel to the coastal region without obtaining an R.C.M.P. permit.

The construction boom sweeping Vancouver in the postwar era brought with it a more liberal attitude toward East Indians. There were jobs aplenty and, although not relishing their presence, white British Columbians showed more tolerance.

The immigration restrictions loosened but not that much. An annual quota of 150 East Indian admissions was adopted in 1951 and six years later the quota was doubled. In 1962 the points system was introduced, replacing the highly discriminatory quota method. All immigration applicants are now approved or rejected on the basis of education, age, skill, language proficiency and other qualifications. Fifty out of a possible 100 points assures entry.

The biggest postwar revision of our immigration policy occurred in 1967, when Parliament endorsed a system permitting foreigners to come here as visitors and to apply for landed-immigrant status from within the country. The system failed. While 7,000 East Indians entered Canada legally that year, untold thousands of white and nonwhite foreigners came in illegally. No longer obliged to stay in their native lands while their immigration papers were being processed, they flocked to Canada by the planeload, then vanished underground.

Last year Ottawa moved to plug the illegal-alien gap and to slow down legal immigration until the Immigration Act could be revamped. All immigrants, regardless of color, race or country of origin, must have a job lined up before they enter Canada, or else they must be "nominated" by a relative already living here. We are presently in the midst of a national debate that will shape our future immigration policy. The alternatives include retention of the points method, a country-of-origin quota system and an annual global ceiling.

Whatever course Ottawa takes, the East Indians will not be leaving South Vancouver. With 90 percent of British Columbia's East Indians belonging to the Sikh religion, an enormous Sikh Temple, the largest structure of its kind outside of India, rivets them to the area.

Like the Jewish synagogue, the Sikh temple has evolved as a community center as well as a religious institution. Social, economic and political matters are openly discussed, frequently at feed-ins in temple basements. The founder of Sikhism, a wandering guru named Nanak Davi, prescribed a unique religious service: congregations are held from Friday evening to Sunday noon, the worshippers taking turns chanting sections of the Granth Sahib until all 1,460 pages are recited.

The whites fighting their residency know nothing of the importance of the temple to the Sikhs. Nor do they care to know. To them, the Sikhs must be forced out because there is a dire housing shortage and the Punjabis are filling precious jobs during a serious employment slump. The whites vow to push them harder, the Sikhs swear they will push back. The specter of an all-out race war stalks the suburb.

South Vancouver is not the only B.C. community troubled by racial tension. Eggs and rocks have been thrown at East Indian homes in Marpole, Surrey, North Vancouver and Burnaby. A Richmond Sikh, coming out of his $60,000 house one morning, found his car splashed with paint. In a northern lumber town, Quesnel, whites and East Indians have clashed in beer parlor brawls.

The situation in British Columbia is shocking and repulsive. Making it even uglier is the reality that this is not the first time the province has experienced a racial flare-up and, judging by the historical evidence, Canada is every bit as capable of nurturing the sort of blatant discrimination we so righteously condemn the American South for practicing against the black minority.

There have been racial incidents in Ontario, Quebec and Nova Scotia too. Any Canadian city, alarmed by the accelerating growth of a nonwhite ghetto in a traditionally white sector, will breed a hoodlum element expressing in physical terms what the majority of the whites are thinking.

Fortunately, not all B.C. Sikhs have been locked out of the white man's world. After their fathers and grandfathers sweated hard in the lumber industry, doing everything from piling planks to selling firewood door-to-door, some East Indians went to university and eventually infiltrated the legal, medical and business professions. Shunning the ghettos, they live in overwhelmingly white middle- or upper middle-class suburbs. They have white friends, they eat Western food, they dress fashion- ably, and many wear turbans only when attending temple ceremonies. With an aptitude H. H. Stevens and the exclu- sionists had thought impossible, they have assimilated.

But they are a small minority. For most B.C. Sikhs, life consists of a laboring job in an often hostile outside environment and Punjabi food, language and family customs in the home. Yet the cold unfriendliness of a foreign land is not going to drive them away. They are determined to endure the hardships until they are accepted and respected—until, in fact, Canada is no longer a white man's country.

Bibliography

Unpublished Sources

BORDEN, Robert L.   Papers, Public Archives of Canada, Ottawa.
BURRELL, Martin.   Papers, Public Archives of Canada, Ottawa.
HUNT, Peter R.   "Sir Richard McBride," masters' degree thesis, U.B.C., 1953, Vancouver Public Library.
LOWES, George.   "The Sikh of British Columbia," graduating essay, U.B.C., 1972.
McBRIDE, Richard.   Papers, Public Archives of B.C., Victoria.
PANNU, Gurdial Singh.   "Sikhs in Canada," thesis, U.B.C., 1970.
STEVENS, H. H.   Private documents. Also Stevens Papers, City Archives, Vancouver.

Public Documents

House of Commons Debates, No. 2457, Ottawa, 1912.

House of Commons Debates, No. 1233, Ottawa, 1914.

House of Commons Sessional Paper, No. 36A, Ottawa, 1914.

Immigration Department file on *Komagata Maru* (RG 76, No. 879545), 1914; Governor General's file on *Komagata Maru* (RG 7), 1914; Department of External Affairs file on *Komagata Maru* (RG 25), 1914; all Public Archives of Canada, Ottawa.

"Report of the Calcutta Committee of Inquiry on the Budge Budge Riot," *Gazette of India*, Delhi, January, 1915.

Report on Immigration to Canada from the Orient and Immigration from India in Particular, W. L. Mackenzie King, Deputy Minister of Labor, King's Printer, Ottawa, 1908.

Report of the Royal Commission on Chinese and Japanese Immigration. Sessional Paper No. 54, Ottawa, 1902.

Report of Special Commissioner H. C. Clogstoun. Submitted to Canadian Government, November 5, 1915.

Report on the Standard of Living of the Orientals of British Columbia. W. A. Carrothers, Victoria, 1935.

U.S. Congressional Record, 63rd Congress, Session II, Appendix, pp. 842–845, Washington, D.C., 1914.

Newspapers and Periodicals

Aryan,   Victoria, 1911.

B.C. Historical Quarterly,   Vancouver, 1941, 1943.

Canadian Business,   Toronto, 1952.

Citizen,   Ottawa, 1914.

Colonist,   Victoria, 1878, 1910, 1914, 1963.

Ghadr,   San Francisco, 1913, 1914, 1916.

Globe,   Toronto, 1914.

Herald,   Lethbridge, 1907.

Hindustanee,   Vancouver, 1914.

Journal, Edmonton, 1907.

Khalsa Herald, Vancouver, 1911.

Maclean's Magazine, Toronto, 1958.

Maclean's Leisure Guide, Vancouver, 1973.

Mercury, Shanghai, 1914.

Monetary Times, Toronto, 1912.

News-Advertiser, Vancouver, 1914.

News-Herald, Vancouver, 1951.

Norseman, Vancouver, 1921.

Pacific Historical Review, San Francisco, 1948, 1969.

Pacific Monthly, Portland, 1907.

Pall Mall Gazette, London, 1914.

Pioneer Mail, Allahabad, 1914.

Province, Vancouver, 1910, 1914, 1950.

Raincoast Chronicles, Vancouver, 1972.

Report, Canadian Historical Association publication, Ottawa, 1936.

Sansar, Victoria, 1912.

Saturday Night, Toronto, 1910.

Second Echo of Ghadr, San Francisco, 1916.

Sun, Vancouver, 1907, 1914, 1943, 1947, 1953.

Times, Victoria, 1910, 1914.

Times, London, 1914.

Victoria Week, Victoria, 1907, 1912.

Westminster Hall Magazine, Vancouver, 1914.

World, Vancouver, 1912, 1914.

World, New York, 1914.

Published Sources

ALLEN, Ralph. *Ordeal by Fire: Canada 1910-1945*. Toronto, Doubleday Canada Ltd., 1961.

ALLEN, Stephen. "Chinatown, My Chinatown," *Maclean's Leisure Guide*, March, 1973.

ANON. "Canada as a Hindu Saw It," *Hindustanee*, 1914.

ANON. "German Plot Bared in Voyage of the Komagata Maru," *Vancouver Sun*, March, 1943.

BEGG, Alexander. *History of British Columbia from Its Earliest Discovery to the Present Time.* Toronto, William Briggs, 1894.

BERTON, Pierre. *The Last Spike: The Great Railway 1881-1885.* Toronto, McClelland and Stewart, 1971.

BORDEN, Henry, Editor. *Robert Laird Borden: His Memoirs. Vol. I (1854-1915).* Toronto, McClelland and Stewart, 1938.

BOUTILIER, Helen. "Vancouver's Earliest Days," *B.C. Historical Quarterly*, April, 1946.

BROWN, Gilles T. "The Hindu Conspiracy, 1914-1917," *Pacific Historical Review*, 1948.

CASHMAN, Tony. *An Illustrated History of Western Canada.* Edmonton, Hurtig Publishers, 1971.

CLARK, Cecil. "Assassins Cut Bloody Trail," *Victoria Colonist*, July 7, 1963.

CREIGHTON, Donald. *Canada's First Century (1867-1967).* Toronto, The Macmillan Company, 1970.

DHARMI, Sadhu Singh. *The Sikhs and Their Religion: A Struggle for Democracy.* Vancouver, published by the Khalsa Diwan Society , 1943.

DHARMAVIRA. *Lala Har Dayal and the Revolutionary Movements of His Times.* New Delhi, Indian Book Company, 1970.

FOOTE, Albert. "The Battle of Burrard Inlet," *Vancouver Sun*, July 19, 1947.

FRANCIS, R. A. "B.C.'s Turbaned Tribe," *Canadian Business*, February, 1952.

GARDEN, Leslie. "Bricks Flew in the Battle of Burrard," *Vancouver Sun*, December 19, 1953.

GARDNER, Ray. "When Vancouver Turned Back the Sikhs," *Maclean's Magazine*, November 8, 1958.

GRAY, James H. *Booze*, Toronto, The Macmillan Co., 1972.

GRIFFITH, W. L. *The Dominion of Canada.* London, Sir Isaac Pitman, 1911.

GUPTA, Manmathnath. *Indian Revolutionary Movement.* Bombay, Somaiya Publications, 1972.

GREGSON, Harry. *A History of Victoria: 1842-1970*. Victoria, Morriss Printing Company, 1970.

HARDY, W. G. *From Sea Unto Sea*. Toronto, Doubleday Canada Ltd., 1959.

HESS, Gary R. "The Hindu in America," *Pacific Historical Review*, 1969

HOWAY, F. W. *British Columbia: The Making of a Province*. Toronto, The Ryerson Press, 1928.

HOLDERNESS, T. W. *Peoples and Problems of India*. London, Williams and Norgate, 1910.

HUTCHISON, Bruce. *The Fraser*. Toronto, Clarke, Irwin and Company Ltd., 1950.

JAIN, Sushil Kumar. "East Indians in Canada," booklet published by P. H. Klop, The Hague, 1971.

KETTLE, Captain. *Western Shores*. Vancouver, Progress Publishing Co. Limited, 1933.

LEACOCK, Stephen. *Canada, The Foundations of the Future*. Montreal, The House of Seagram, 1941.

LOCKLEY, Fred. "The Hindu Invasion," *Pacific Monthly*, Vol. 17, 1907.

MATHUR, L. P. *Indian Revolutionary Movement in the United States of America*. New Delhi, S. Chand, 1970.

McCAFFREY, Peggy. "Towboating," *Raincoast Chronicles*, Madeira Park, B.C., Autumn, 1972.

McCURDY, James. *Marine History of the Pacific Northwest*. Seattle, Superior Publishing Company, 1966.

McGREGOR, D. A. "On a Summer Day, 1914," *Vancouver Province*, August 5, 1950.

McKELVIE, B. A. *Magic, Murder and Mystery*. Cobble Hill, B.C., Cowichen-Leader Printing Company, 1966.

MORLEY, Alan. *Vancouver: From Milltown to Metropolis*. Vancouver, Mitchell Press, 1961.

MORSE, Eric. "Some Aspects of the Komagata Maru Affair, 1914," *Report*, Canadian Historical Association, 1936.

NICOL, Eric. *Vancouver*. Toronto, Doubleday Canada Ltd., 1970.

NORRIS, John. *Strangers Entertained: A History of the Ethnic Groups of British Columbia*. Vancouver, Evergreen Press, 1971.

ONDAATJE, Christopher, and Robert Catherwood. *The Prime Ministers of Canada 1867-1967*. Toronto, Canyon Press, 1967.

REID, Robie L. "The Inside Story of the Komagata Maru," *B.C. Historical Quarterly*, January, 1941.

ROBIN, Martin. *The Rush for the Spoils 1871-1933: The Company Province, Vol. I*. Toronto, McClelland and Stewart, 1972.

SANFORD, D. A. *Leaves from the Journal of a Subaltern During the Campaign in the Punjab, Sept. 1848–March 1849*. London, William Blackwood and Sons, 1849.

SCOTT, W. D. "Immigration and Population," *Canada and Its Provinces, Vol. 7*. Toronto, Glasgow, Brook and Company, 1914.

SINGH, Gurdit. *The Voyage of the Komagata Maru*. Published privately in Calcutta during the 1920s.

SINGH, Khushwant. *A History of the Sikhs, Vol. I (1469-1839) and Vol II (1839-1964)*. New Jersey, Princeton University Press, 1966.

STEVENS, H. H. "Should British Columbia Admit The Hindu," *Monetary Times*, February 17, 1912.

TUCKER, Gilbert N. "The Career of the H.M.C.S. Rainbow," *B.C. Historical Quarterly*, January, 1943.